# The Danagla Traders of Northern Sudan

To my children:
Sami, Mona, Husham and Talal

# The Danagla Traders of Northern Sudan

Rural Capitalism & Agricultural Development

**El Haj Bilal Omer**

Ithaca Press London 1985

First published in 1985 by
Ithaca Press 13 Southwark Street London SE1 1RU
Typeset by
EMS Photosetters Rochford Essex
Printed in England by
Biddles Ltd Guildford & King's Lynn

Omer, El Haj Bilal
The Danagla traders of northern Sudan.——(Sudan studies series; no. 10)
1. Danagla (African people)——Social conditions
2. Danagla (African people)——Economic conditions
I. Title II. Series
305.8'9625 DT155.2.D/

ISBN 0-86372-029-3

# CONTENTS

# List of Tables



# List of Figures

# Introduction

After an anthropological study of a Danagla village, Mushu, in 1974/5, many questions arose as to the process of agricultural development in the area which was beyond the scope of the first research. I developed an interest in the causes which contributed to the transformation of the Danagla peasant economy as it was in the period just before and after the Re-Conquest of the country in 1898, to the type of economy which is more and more becoming capitalist in the sense of the increasing role of capital in changing what was once a subsistence economy. I had a faint idea about the determinant factors on the development of the present socio-economic structures; basically these were premised on the prevailing production relations and their gradual change from those constituted in the kinship relations to those seemingly individualistic, secularized and commercial relations of production of today as seen in the different forms of share-cropping practised in the area. A possible determinant cause was sought in the activities of local entrepreneurs especially traders whose activities have had an important role in the agricultural developments and the economy of the area.

To study a region whose population is scattered over a vast number of villages and settlements along the river banks, in oases which are difficult to reach with conventional means of transport, and in the basins which have contributed a lot to the heterogeneity of the region, it was difficult to select a representative unit. Instead, I adopted a different approach which allowed for wider coverage of the region as a whole.

Since I was concerned with the agricultural development I found it plausible to focus on one important dynamic factor in bringing about changes affecting that development – that is capital. In an arid zone the necessity for irrigation presupposes relatively large investment resources, and hence the focus on the process of capital accumulation within the peasant economy and also trading profits and their reinvestment in agriculture and trade.

The study of the class of traders, the small shopkeepers scattered throughout the villages, and wholesalers who are concentrated in the towns, allowed me a better chance of covering the whole region as a geographical entity and seeing the local differences in the forms of economic and social organization. The methods used were mainly documentary sources, interview schedules, life-histories and case studies. Sampling for the interviews (one for the study of pump schemes and one for the traders) posed a difficulty as the records did not give the real number of traders in the area. The mode of selection of the sample from the traders for study is described in Chapter Six. The object of interviewing the traders was to collect basic demographic data and to elucidate their activities past and present in agricultural investment. This necessitated conducting these interviews mostly by myself as the life histories of some of those interviewed were documented as well. From these, most of the information on the history of trade, credit relations and development and organization of co-operatives was collected. Documents and case studies are mostly utilized in Chapters Two and Four regarding the history of the area and its population and the developments in the material means of production.

However, non-traders and government officials provided me with indispensable information or helped to introduce me to potential informants on the history of the region, and its social organization especially the elderly informants without whose help it would be very difficult to document the recent history of otherwise neglected aspects of these people's life.

## Acknowledgements

I am much indebted to my hosts, the Danagla, whose help and co-operation enabled me to conduct the research on which this book is based. To their elders, to their traders, and local officials in all departments, I owe my thanks and gratitude which I hope can be realized in more practical participation in the advancement of this part of the country.

My special thanks are to the University of Khartoum for the grant and facilities offered to finish this work; to Professor Yusuf Fadl Hassan, Director of the Institute of African and Asian Studies for his assistance and support; to the Economic and Social Research Council for its financial help.

And in Hull: my thanks to my supervisors, Dr Talal Asad for his guidance in the early stages; and to Professor Ian Cunnison who supervised, criticized and commented on my work in the most tedious and demanding stage of writing, without whose guidance, encouragement and patience this would have been a difficult task to finish. My thanks to Teresa Weatherston and Eileen Lee for typing the manuscript in the most disturbing and disruptive conditions.

Finally, my special thanks to my family, especially my mother, Hawa, my brother Abdul Azim and my wife, Su'ad, who gave me considerable support and encouragement.

## A Note on Transliteration

I have tried to use as few Arabic or Nubian words as possible, but for certain words which can only be translated at some length, I preferred to use them as they are used locally; these mostly concern agricultural activity and implements. A glossary (Appendix I) is attached giving the nearest equivalent meanings for the words used.

For phonological transliteration I have followed the system used in *Sudan Notes and Records* except for geographical places which have conventional ways of writing them used by the Survey Department of the Democratic Republic of the Sudan.

# Danagla Homeland

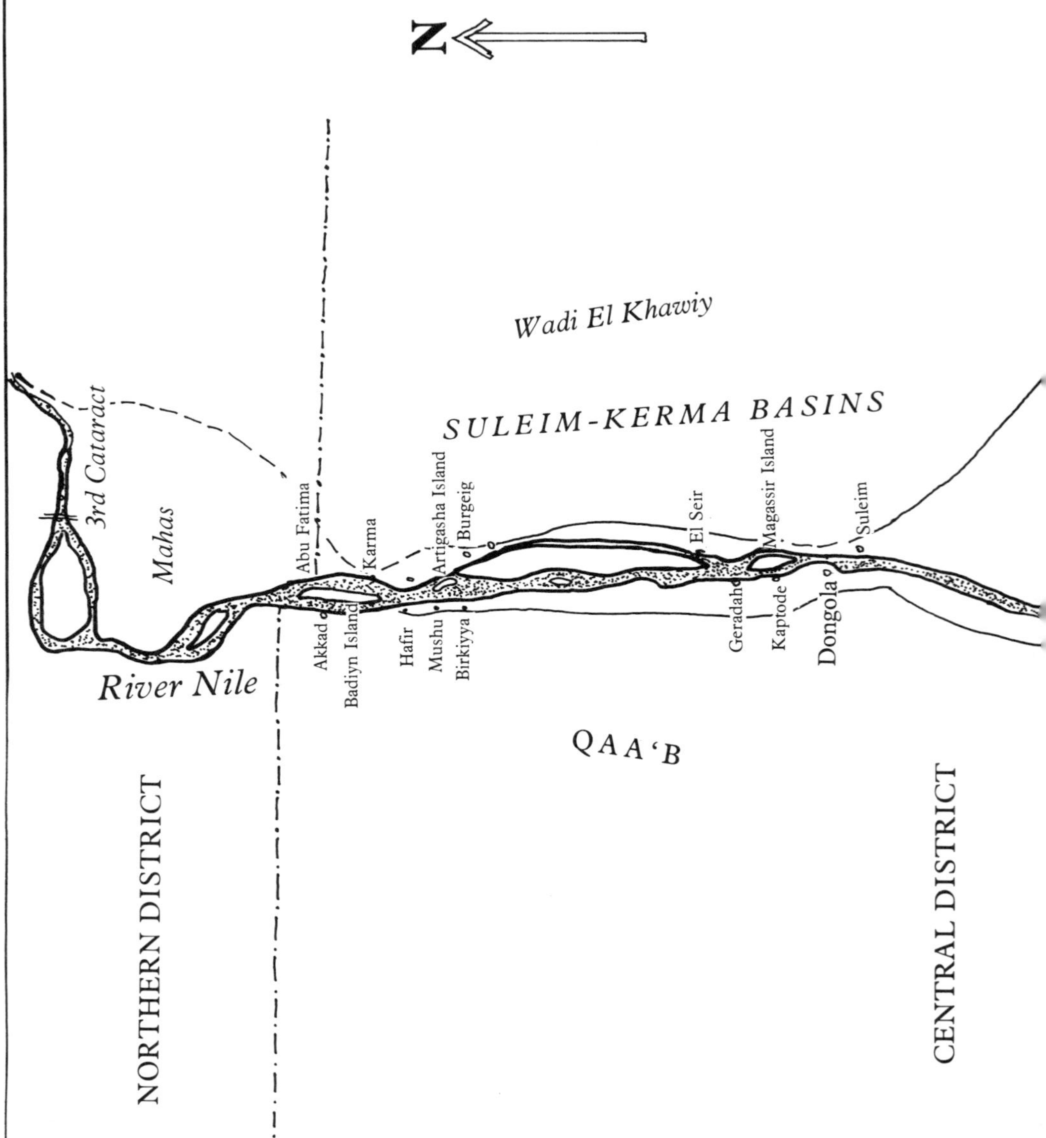

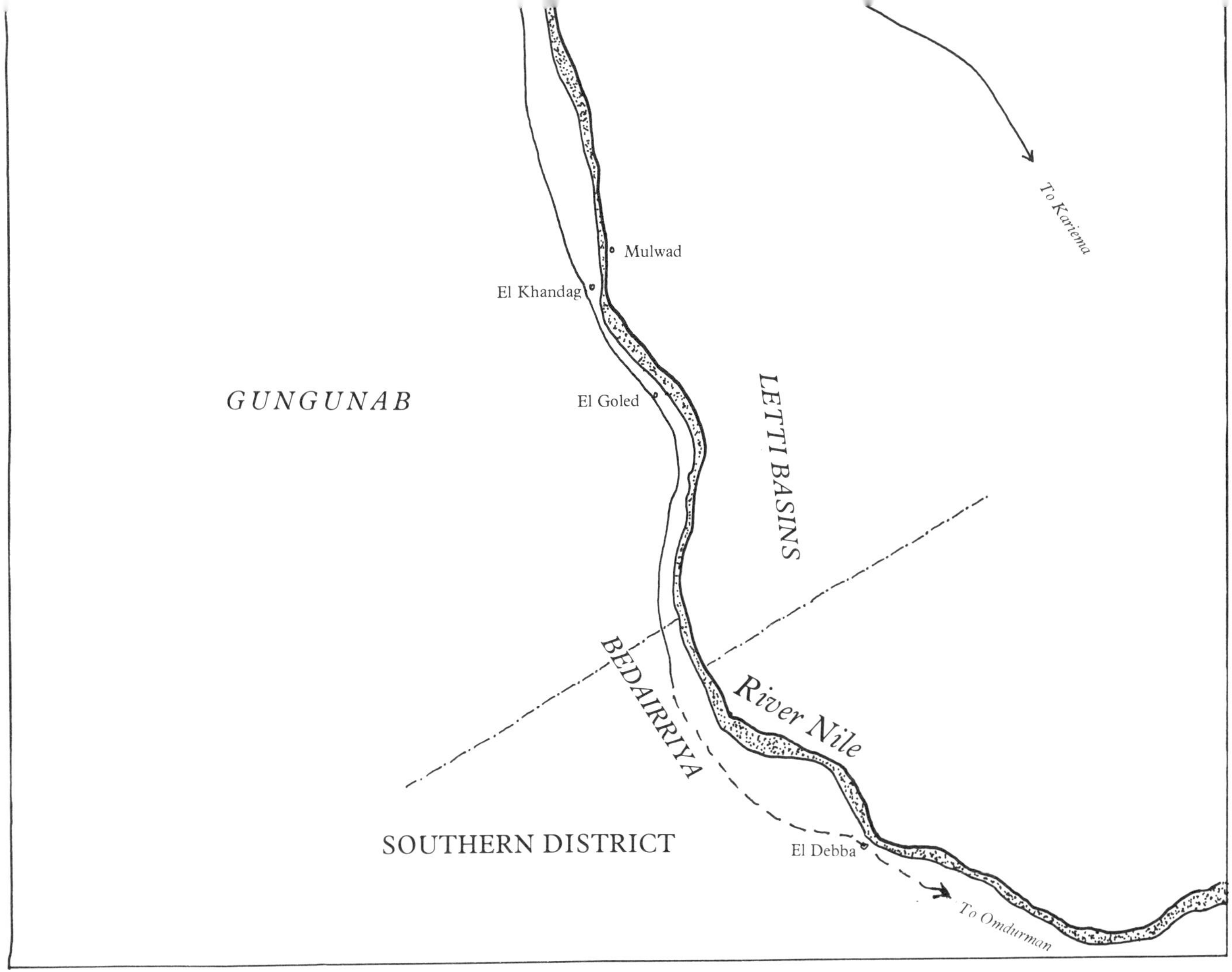

To Kariema
Mulwad
El Khandag
El Goled
GUNGUNAB
LETTI BASINS
BEDAIRRIYA
River Nile
SOUTHERN DISTRICT
El Debba
To Omdurman

# Chapter One: Introduction

## A. Colonialism, Dependency and Development:

In recent anthropological studies there are a number of issues arising from the sub-title above. The debates seem to be inconclusive and many of the recent discussions have added to the confusions over the definitions of concepts and categories relating to the socio-economic structures in the countries of the Third World. The main difference lies between those who adhere to the analysis of 'dual' structures within these countries, and those who do not accept such an approach and maintain an analysis which adheres to the integration of the economies with that of the industrial capitalist countries.[1] Within the latter group, there are different approaches which try to discern the nature of the processes in this integration, and how it is achieved and maintained to serve the interests of capitalism. Such an exercise has produced divergent views on definitions and analytical frameworks. The rejection of the 'dualism' approach and modernization theories required substitute explanatory models for the existing non-capitalist socio-economic formations and different modes of production, as well as a redefinition of capitalism itself.[2] The major differences seem to centre on the questions of specifying the nature of the economies influenced by the developed capitalism of the West and also the nature of the dependency relationships between capitalist countries and those of the Third World.

The development or underdevelopment of these dependent economies is determined by their relation with the capitalist economies and consequently these economies respond, or otherwise are coerced to respond, to the requirements of capitalism; and in that process they themselves undergo changes compatible with the demands of the dominant economy. However, a combination of coercive and non-coercive forces worked in certain parts of the Third World depending on the capitalist strategic necessities which are partially fulfilled through international trade or, failing that, through direct subjugation and colonization as was the case in most African countries south of the Sahara.

In the Sudan, forms of development have been different from those in other former colonies. There have been also different forms within the Sudan, and this implies the parts coexistence of different structures. If we accept the Frankian thesis that the remotest of the Third World have been integrated into the structure of the metropolis, that their structures are increasingly becoming capitalist, and that the differences which manifest themselves are not significant, then the Sudan's diversity poses a challenge to this position. Nevertheless the domination of capitalism has not yet been established to such an extent as to render the precapitalist modes of production obsolete. In some parts of Southern and Western Sudan, for example, it would be sheer speculation to talk about capitalist penetration in any form.

The dependency relationship can only be established when we look at the requirements of western capitalism through the activities of the colonial government, as were demonstrated in the production of cotton especially in the Gezira. This followed the subordination of the country to the British Empire in 1899 when the country came again under colonial rule in the Anglo-Egyptian Condominium.[3] The country was coercively brought under the domination of capitalism by the fact that it was conquered. The interests of the government later were identical with those of industrial capital in England. The imposition of cash crops, mainly cotton, on the indigenous systems of production and on the forms of organization introduced (especially in the Gezira) with local compromises produced what could be referred to as partially capitalist and partially pre-capitalist organizations. Describing the resultant system in the Gezira, Tony Barnett wrote:

> However it does not itself constitute a capitalist system of production; it is not characterised by the exclusive use of free wage-labour. Rather, it consists of a whole range of productive relationships, some of which are very close to free wage-labour, and others of which are quite far removed from this form of organization.[4]

However, the impact of the capitalist system on the previous systems of production in the Gezira and the other areas where the government undertook similar endeavours is discernable and increasingly developed its capitalistic nature, though in different manifestations. If the Sudan is taken as a whole, then we can speak of sectors or 'pockets' where capitalism has had an influence. Mainly there are systems of production which are non-capitalist coexisting with the penetrating capitalist forms of organization. The transformation of these systems does not wholly depend on the expansion of capitalism and its relations of production; internal factors are very important in hastening or impeding such development. Although production in the Gezira scheme was tied mainly to the requirements of the textile industry in England, that did not necessitate the total imposition of capitalist relations of production. These developed gradually after a period of coexisting with the previous forms and subsequently they have seemed to dominate, though even today not fully.

In the areas where direct measures (namely the construction of big irrigation works for specifically planned production) were not used, previous forms of production continued to exist and have been changing in response to factors other than some of those working in the Gezira. Capitalism then, can co-exist with incompatible forms of production, adapt them to its requirements, or opt for outright destruction of these forms. This view has been the dominant theme in a special issue of the *Review of African Political Economy* where it was stated that:

> . . . capitalism developed in some cases by eliminating non-capitalist forms of production, in other cases by adapting them to the requirements of capitalism and in yet others by developing new forms of production to serve its needs.[5]

Further they added:

> . . . the old modes have been co-opted to serve new ends. Peasants continue to produce under non-capitalist modes even as they are co-opted into the international economy.[6]

In the view of these contributors it is contended that once a country is brought under capitalist domination or penetration then its working, adaptation, adjustment and transformation become viewed only from the interests of capitalism. Similar positions were taken by others but at least they allowed for a secondary role for the non-capitalist forms to change themselves; Barbara Bradby attributed such a role to the indigenous forms:

> . . . The expanded reproduction of capitalism resulted in the articulation of the capitalist mode of production with 'pre-capitalist' modes. The nature of this articulation and its consequences for the pre-capitalist mode of production is a function first and predominantly, of the needs of the capitalist mode of production and second of the internal structure of the pre-capitalist mode.[7]

Earlier, in 1971, Frank had expressed a similar view but did not accord the pre-capitalist modes any significance and depicted them as not fundamental.[8] Others, e.g. J. Ennew, allowed a measure of autonomous development and although constrained by the logic of capitalism not necessarily imposed:

> The capitalist system of production subordinates other forms of possession and other labour processes by integrating them into its processes of exchange, and, through circulation, imposes on them the logic of its process of production.[9]

From the brief review above it is evident that there is a trend in recent studies to take for granted the expansion tendency as well as the dominance of capitalism; this seems to perpetuate an analysis which largely neglects the independent tendencies towards transformation within pre-capitalist economies and the question of how it comes about.

In this study I will attempt an analysis of different patterns of development in the economy of the Central District of the Northern Province of the Sudan (See Map I). The peculiar position of the region together with its different geographical, social and economic characteristics would suggest many differences from those in the Gezira. The analysis of these differences and their effects on its development requires detailed investigation of specific processes of changes taking place in the region. A major difference as regards development is that the colonial government influenced the changes in the Gezira whereas in the Northern Province developments have been largely induced by local factors. The province did not constitute a source of raw materials for capitalist industries, nor was it easy to make any major agricultural investments because the province is mostly desertland with negligible rainfall. Agriculture here depends totally on irrigation from the main Nile; and hence the need for sufficient resources to provide irrigation equipment. The lack of government intervention with the Danagla economy has been observed before. Thornton stated flatly that his interest in studying the Northern Province:

> . . . comes from the fact that it is the one part of the Sudan which has begun to change from a subsistence to a substantially commercial character without the direct intervention of government with large-scale agricultural planning.[10]

Later, in 1975, a similar remark was made by the experts of the ILO:

> Until recently development in the Sudan was directed only to the modern sector agriculture and industry which imply concentration in Central Kordofan and by-passing traditional agriculture, small-scale manufacturing

> and the regions of the country which are already lagging behind the growth poles of greater Khartoum and the triangle between the Blue and White Nile.[11]

A major question is this: if the government has not intervened substantially then, what are the forces which have caused this substantial change – a change which is comparable to that in the areas where the government has had a direct role? In a situation when the colonial government was the major agent for investment in the country, the Northern Province was left to its own devices and hence showed a different course of development from that in the Gezira although the resultant forms can be explained, as those of the Gezira can, within the context of capitalist expansion. The province's development, instead of being influenced by the working of industrial capital extending itself as productive capital as was the case in the Gezira, was achieved by primitive accumulation in agriculture and the working of local trade whose relationship with the international market in the past can hardly be established except for the few and limited relations with Egypt which will be described in Chapter 6.

Thornton's statement above suggests lack of planning and also lack of direct investment, but the Government has yet an important role to play without, however, directly affecting the structure of the local economy and its relations of production. Its role can be understood when we look at its land registration, and its licensing and taxation laws formulated to encourage those who possessed the necessary resources to embark on agricultural investment. It was a major policy of the early administration to encourage foreigners, especially Egyptian pensioners, to come and invest in the province's agriculture, but the policy was unsuccessful.[12] Thus the government provided the conditioning factors for the increase in the region's production and left actual investment to the working of local entrepreneurs, especially traders.

In the first thirty years following the Re-Occupation the main activity of the government was the pacification of the country and the settlement of people after a period of war and national upheavals. Compared to the next thirty years, the first thirty were a period of direct investment to provide the settled population with enough grain. In 1909 the Suleim basin scheme was started for the production of fodder and more importantly to contribute to the settlement of the Danagla who were showing a high rate of out-migration. In 1916 the colonial government established a number of pump schemes along the Nile to provide subsistence crops and supply fodder for the British cavalry regiments in Egypt.[13] But none of these schemes was in the area under study. After 1936, the governing partners of the Sudan, Britain and Egypt, disagreed in their policies towards the Sudan. This resulted in the withdrawal of Egypt from its financial commitments towards the Condominium. The colonial government started a self-sufficiency policy as regards finance and investment because the British government was not in a position to spare any resources towards the administration and development of the Condominium,[14] nor were the western firms interested in the whole country as the activities of The Sudan Plantations Syndicate demonstrate.[15] So new laws allowing for the acquisition of government land, tax exemptions and other concessions were enacted to encourage private investors, nationals and foreigners. In the mid-thirties and during the Second World War an important trend started in the region following the boom in the prices of agricultural products. This was a turning point for mercantile capital as it transferred itself partially into productive capital by the involvement of traders in agricultural investment. However, a limited expansion of the peasant production of the area was just sufficient to meet the exchange requirements of market goods introduced by trade from Egypt, and gradually the peasant economy became more and more geared to the production of commodities for exchange in outside markets, especially the production of cash crops. By reaching this stage, the relations of the economy with capitalism can be seen in the working of the regional, national and international trade.

**B General Characteristics of the Danagla Economy:**

The categories 'peasants' and 'peasant economies' have attracted much attention since the work of Redfield (1956) in Central America. Attempts have been made to redefine his concepts but so far these seem to be not sufficient to provide the concepts for the study of rural agrarian societies. The works of Wolf (1966, 1969), Dalton (1971), Shanin (1973), Mintz (1973) and others put them in a position that advocates the possibility of defining peasantries as historical entities within broader frameworks of encompassing wholes yet with structures and mechanisms of their own.[16] A recent position regards the peasantries as inseparable from the encapsulating wholes and understandable only in the context of the analysis of these wholes. This position is represented by works like that of Harrison (1977), Ennew et.al. (1977) and Roseberry (1978).[2]

Some of the latter group have by-passed the difficulties in definitions and accepted a general trend in viewing peasantries as transitional categories of agrarian petty producers integrated with the larger political, economic and social wholes. Some would not accept the value of studying them before studying the larger societies of which they form a part. Roseberry, for example, wrote:

> If peasants exist within larger societies, let us begin with those societies, examine the social, political and economic processes of development (or underdevelopment) which are at work in them, and then analyse rural regions in terms of those larger processes. The problem of articulation disappears because we are no longer talking about two discrete units which somehow are related but about a total society.[18]

Moreover he suggests the dropping of the concepts yet retaining microsociological studies:

> This essay does not suggest that we abandon microsociological studies of peasant producers, but it does contend that we must drop all notions of peasant society or economy.[19]

Others have just dropped the notions altogether or assumed an accepted definition for granted. Harrison, for example, wrote:

> Whether they are defined as the immediate producers who own the means of production, or as the family household operating its farm with non-wage family labour, we know, generally speaking, who the peasants are.[20]

In an earlier paper on the definition of peasants, Sidney Mintz contended that the typology of peasantries according to specific measurable characteristics is important in that it makes it possible for controlled comparison; whereas recapitulation of the differences in definition serves no useful purpose.[21] However in my work on the Danagla, I did not give much attention to the different definitions suggested. I do not think I would escape the complexities involved in characterization and definition. Nevertheless I have used the term peasant in two different senses: the first when describing a situation when the cultivator owned his means of production and relied totally on his family labour and the co-operation of fellow peasants on a reciprocal basis, and the different situation at present where the the cultivator controls his labour only; the second sense used when describing a situation including both peasant farmer and tenant farmer with small holdings.

However, I believe that the Danagla economy has specific characteristics in its production relations and also in its exchange relationships which have proved to exist within different forms of economic and social organization. Such a position will place this study within the traditional approach of treating them as a 'society', 'economy', etc. but at the same time I will make clear the level at which this economy articulates with the society at large or other forms of relations with similar societies or economies. In Wolf (1966) we find that reference to the articulation of different structures is implicit in his 'fund of rent' though not specified. He used the 'fund of rent' as the defining characteristic of the peasant economy but the chain of appropriators and the means of siphoning it were not fully analysed beyond the local powers.

> . . . when someone exercises an effective superior power, or domain, over a cultivator, the cultivator must produce a fund of rent. It is this fund of rent which critically distinguishes the peasant from the primitive cultivator . . . It is important to note, though, that there are many different ways in which this fund of rent is produced and many ways in which it is siphoned from the peasant stratum into the hands of the controlling groups.[22]

Although this statement does not specify the controlling groups, Shanin on the other hand has specified them as, in addition to landlords, other social groups which have shares through rent, interest on loans, tax, etc.[23]

However my work will not formulate a definition for 'peasant' or 'peasant economy'; instead it contributes to add to the existing variations of peasantries by showing a different type of economy and the stress on the exchange relations which integrate it with other economies. A major concern will be the analysis of the internal dynamics of development in the Danagla economy and how the economy reacted to stimuli from within and outside the area.

Until the mid-thirties the community under study approximated to the modal definitions of a peasant economy with specific type of production-consumption units based on family labour. The *sagiya*[24] was the basic unit of economic and social organization within the villages with the agnatic descent group providing both the labour, sometimes by contracting hired labour or using slaves, and the means of irrigation which constituted of the *sagiya* machine and draught animals. Under this system of production we find a form of horizontal organization (see Chapter 5, Section II) where each *sagiya* was an independent unit making its own decisions concerning crops, areas to be cultivated, crop rotations, etc. This presupposes a mode of economic, social and political organization which worked to enhance that system of production, and to a large extent contributed to its survival for a prolonged period. Despite the socio-political changes that influenced the *sagiya* economic base, freehold land (*milk*) and the technical changes which increased agricultural production, yet the relations of production prevailing under the *sagiya* have undergone slight changes. They have continued to exist after major developments in the forces of production and the socio-political changes taking place in the country as a whole. The persistence of these relations will be fully described in Chapter 5.

The expropriation of surpluses from the peasants has never been absent in the different patterns of production in the area under study, yet the appropriators have been changing over time; as has the organization of the peasants. The former autonomy of the peasant household-labour unit (the *sagiya*) has disappeared from the sphere of production and more individualization is taking place there as we can see from the analysis later (Chapter 5).

The big technical changes, especially those affecting irrigation (pump schemes); the expansion of the cultivable land; the increasing heterogeneity of the population and the changes in the social division of labour resulting from that, all contributed towards changing the peasant cultivator of the *sagiya* into a tenant cultivator who has no other right but that of realizing his labour in the cultivation of land which is controlled by other forces. Yet the manner in which his surplus products are expropriated is not basically different from that under the *sagiya* system (especially situations B and C under the *sagiya*).

The persistence of the *sagiya* relations of production in most of their characteristics, the distribution of products for example, is a defining characteristic of the present Danagla economic organization. Despite the developments in the conditions of production, and the increased commercialization and individualization which are all favourable to the penetration of capitalist relations, the *sagiya* relations still exist and seem to be very resistant to the attempts to change them. Nevertheless there is a tendency for the penetration of capitalist organization – defined basically by the use of free wage-labour – into one sector of agricultural production, namely fruit and vegetables which are produced under conditions different from those of the seasonal crops. Also the penetration started partially in some small farms runs by traders near the towns. The past and present activities of these traders will be analysed, and it will be shown how they influenced the development of the region through their trading activities and their direct involvement in agricultural investment.

## C Mercantile Capital and the transformation of the Peasant Economy:

Development in Dongola area has been largely constrained by the availability of sufficient capital for the installation of modern and efficient irrigation techniques and for the reclamation of cultivable land. The necessary capital for these developments has been provided privately by traders, migrants, co-operatives, etc. as well as from agricultural surpluses accumulated by the peasants. Although this book addresses particularly the analysis of mercantile capital and its accumulation, all forms of accumulation in the region are described with the relationships they have with each other and with the peasant economy.

Merchant capital by definition works outside production since it does not create values. Its domain is circulation, i.e. trade – unless it otherwise gets involved in production incidently. As trading capital it does not influence production on a large scale since its major target is not production but control over the market. This general characteristic applies to merchant capital past and present in capitalist and non-capitalist economies alike:

> Merchants do not make their profits by revolutionizing production but by controlling markets, and the greater the control they are able to exercise, the higher their rate of profit.[25]

The statement by Kay applies to all forms of production, yet the stimulus or influence given to production is always indirect. For merchant capital brings about new needs through expansion of trade, which in turn requires peasant producers to increase their production to secure sufficient surpluses, so as to meet the market exchange requirements. This can be seen from the penetration of Egyptian petty traders in Dongola region: they exchanged food crops for new kinds of items they imported from Egypt. But the effect on peasant production cannot be said to be so great as to demand any change in the techniques of production, the areas under cultivation or the organization of production. The peasants could have saved some of their crops by refraining from consuming them in exchange for these items which were scarce at the start – sugar, tea, salt, perfumes etc. But when other items were introduced, like fine woven cloths and durable items, then gradual expansion have taken place. Marx pointed to this process when he wrote:

> The degree to which the movement towards the establishment of exchange value then attacks the whole of production depends partly on the intensity of this external influence (external trade), and partly on the degree of development attained by the elements of domestic production – division of labour etc.[26]

The same contention has been reiterated by later writers in a way which adds clarification to Marx's view. G. Kay has given a bigger role to merchant capital than that accorded to it by Marx. He gave it a more positive role in influencing the development of internal forces of production:

> By encouraging commodity production which increases the division of labour and stimulates productivity, merchant capital not only plays a positive part in the development of the productive forces of society, it also opens the way for the reorganization of production upon a capitalist basis. But historically merchant capital has never been able to affect this transition to capitalism proper.[27]

The influence of merchant capital on production then is not direct yet it is substantial as it opens the way for re-organization, as Kay claims, on a capitalist basis. More capitalist relations ensue when merchant capital becomes directly involved in production – that is changing itself from circulation capital to productive capital and that depends largely on the profitability of the already existing organization of the system of distribution in the production process. In the present study it is found that although merchant capital has influenced the expansion of agricultural production, improved the conditions of labour and changed the division of labour in society by assuming a different role as productive capital, yet it has not radically influenced the organization of production, which remains similar to that which operated when merchant capital was confined to the sphere of circulation. An important characteristic of productive capital used here is that it is inseparable from purely mercantile capital. Traders do not keep detailed accounts or run their trading businesses and agricultural investments separately. So this situation demands the analysis of productive capital as entangled with merchant capital, although in theory we can separate them for analytical reasons in an artificial way.

The process of capital accumulation took root in the circulation sphere as early as the history of trade in the area suggests. Also some of the wealth, now used as productive capital, has been accumulated within the production sphere itself as some of the peasants were able to accumulate and appropriate surpluses from other peasants. However capital generated from within the peasant economy of subsistence production was different in nature from the one that was introduced, and later regenerated itself, by the alien group of traders coming from outside, especially from Egypt. Both are a consequence of the accumulation of surplus values from the peasants, but as one posited itself in trade, i.e. circulation, the other was located in agriculture, that is the sphere of production. An important point here is that even these surpluses have been passed through the stage of trade, as the middle peasants usually start retail trade as a transitory step together with carrying out cultivation for a considerable period.

Immigrants, originally from Egypt, started their life in the area as craftsmen and share-croppers. After saving enough money to furnish a small hawking business, they would start this petty trade and gradually expand their range of work and accumulate more wealth. So the process of capital accumulation even for those migrants has taken root locally. In its first stages as I have said, merchant capital was confined to the sphere of circulation, and had very limited influence on peasant production. Traders in the Dongola area until the 1930s were not involved in production and they could only provide the peasants with items that they could not provide themselves. Sugar, tea, fine woven cloths, perfumes and cooking utensils, i.e. market goods, were the items the peasants needed and these could only be provided from Egypt or later from national markets. The introduction of these items led the peasants to produce more than their stable grain requirements to furnish the exchange equivalent of these market goods. They had to exchange their grain directly for these market goods (barter) or otherwise sell their grain and with the money therefrom purchase these goods. Appropriation of the peasant surpluses was different from that in the present situation where traders were directly appropriating surpluses not only in the sphere of circulation as profits on goods supplied, but also by direct appropriation of surplus production. Merchant capital has assumed a different role, and changed at least partly into productive capital. By making such a change the traders get two-fold profits; from the marketing of the peasants' products, and this lies in the sphere of circulation; and the marketing of their own shares accruing to them as interest and profits from the employment of their capital in the production sphere. So they increase the surpluses expropriated from the peasants not only extensively[28] by bringing more land under cultivation but also intensively by introducing advanced techniques and new crops; and by controlling the marketing of the crops. The processes of change from circulation to production will be analysed in Chapter 6.

This book addresses itself to the analysis of the processes involved in the development of the Danagla economy, that is its transformation from a characteristically subsistence economy to one oriented to commodity production and articulated through different levels with capital. In Chapter Two the social structure of the Danagla with their different ethnic composition which to a large extent obscures the formation of social classes based on the positioning in the production process, is described together with the history of settlement of the different groups. In Chapter Three the structure of the peasant family is discussed in relation to development in the forces of production and the changes in the division of labour in the society. Chapter Four analyses the means of production, land, labour and capital and the different changes these have experienced over the last seventy years and their impact on the expansion of production. Chapter Five looks into the different forms of production relations, the process of capital accumulation and its circulation, and the distribution of agricultural products. Special attention is paid to the technical developments, which have revolutionized the forces of production and contributed to the increase of peasant production. However, the effects on the distribution system are minimal despite the efforts of the government and co-operatives to change them. Two different sets of production relations are described here, the Suleim Basin and Burgeig government scheme for comparison with the private schemes whose relations are basically those prevalent under the *sagiya* system, and this shows different patterns of development in the same region. Chapter Six discusses the merchant class, their constitutions, activities etc. together with the development of trade, rural towns and communication. Also it includes the growth of local markets and their integration with the national and consequently the international markets.

## Notes

1 For comprehensive reviews of the theories and approaches in studying Third World development see the papers by Alejandro Portes, 'On the Sociology of National Development Theories and Issues'; Ronald H. Chilcote; 'Dependency: a Critical Synthesis of the Literature'; Samir Amin, 'Underdevelopment and Dependence in Black Africa – origins and contemporary forms'; Giovanni Arrighi, 'International Corporations, labour aristocracies and economic development in tropical Africa'; in Richard Hay, Jr., and Janet Abu Lughod (editors), *Third World Urbanization*, Chicago, 1977. See also, Long, N., *An Introduction to the Sociology of Rural Development*, Tavistock, 1977, chapters 2 and 4 for the evaluation and differences of the two main approaches.

2 For example Laclau based his criticism of Frank mainly on their different ways of defining capitalism, which in turn initiated long debates. Frank's definition can be simplified by the equation that capitalism = feudalism + market; this runs at variance with Marxian definitions for which feudalism and capitalism are two different modes of production with specific characteristics, whereas Frank's position is too general to differentiate between them in this way.

3 There were of course other reasons for the ReConquest which are beyond the scope of this study.

4 Tony Barnett, *The Gezira Scheme: An Illusion of Development*, MacMillan, 1977, p.23.

5 See Editorial of *Review of African Political Economy*, No. 3, May-October, 1975, p.3.

6 *ibid.*, p.4.

7 Barbara Bradby, 'The Destruction of Natural Economy', *Economy and Society*, Volume 4, No. 2, May 1975, p.127.

8 See A. G. Frank, *Capitalism and Underdevelopment in Latin America*, Penguin, 1971, p.37, where he stated, '. . . Evidently capitalism admits, nay, requires, a variety of such relations corresponding to the variety of capitalist circumstances and development.' See also R. Leaver, 'The Debate on Underdevelopment: on situating Gunder Frank', *Journal of Contemporary Asia*, Vol. 7, No. 1, 1977, p.110.

9 J. Ennew et.al., 'Peasantry as an Economic Category', in *Journal of Peasant Studies*, Vol. 4, No. 4, 1977, p.306.
10 D. S. Thornton, 'Regional Development: the case of the Northern Sudan'; in *Agricultural Development in the Sudan*, Vol. 2, edited D. J. Shaw, Khartoum, p.35.
11 International Labour Office, *Growth, Employment and Equity; A Comprehensive Strategy for the Sudan*, Vol. II, Geneva, 1975, p.5.
12 See Reports on Dongola Province, *Sudan Pamphlets*, No. 15, University of Khartoum, 1897, p.2.
13 J. W. Hewison, Northern Province Agriculture in J. D. Tothill (ed.) *Agriculture in the Sudan*, 1948, p.749.
14 See G. M. Salih, The heritage of local government, in *Local Government and Politics in the Sudan*, edited by J. Howell, Khartoum, 1974, p.15.
15 T. Barnett, *op.cit.*, pp.3–5.
16 Redfield R., *Peasant Society and Culture*, Chicago, 1956; E. Wolf, *Peasants*, Prentice-Hall, 1966. Also, *Peasant Wars of the Twentieth Century*, Faber and Faber 1969; G. Dalton, 'Peasantries in Anthropology and History', *Current Anthropology*, October 1972; S. W. Mintz, 'A Note on the Definition of Peasantries', The *Journal of Peasant Studies*, Vol. 1, No. 1, October 1973, and, T. Shanin, 'The Nature and Logic of the Peasant Economy', *ibid.*
17 J. Ennew, et.al., 'Peasantry as an Economic Category', *The Journal of Peasant Studies*, Vol. 4, No. 4, 1977; M. Harrison, 'The Peasant Mode of Production in the Work of A. V. Chayanov', *ibid.*; and W. Roseberry, 'Peasants as Proletarians', *Critique of Anthropology*, No. 11, 1978.
18 W. Roseberry, 'Peasants as Proletarians', *Critique of Anthropology*, No. 11, 1978, p.3.
19 *Ibid.*, p.3.
20 M. Harrison, 'The Peasant Mode of Production in the Work of A. V. Chayanov', *Journal of Peasant Studies*, Vol. 4, No. 4, 1977, p.323.
21 See S. W. Mintz, 'A Note on the Definition of Peasants', *Journal of Peasant Studies*, Vol. I, No. 1, 1973, p.92.
22 E. Wolf, *Peasants*, Prentice-Hall, 1966, pp.9–10.
23 T. Shanin, 'The Nature and Logic of the Peasant Economy; 1: A Generalization', *The Journal of Peasant Studies*, Vol. I, No. 1, October 1973, p.76.
24 The *sagiya* is an oxen-driven wooden water wheel. The word has three references according to the context; a) the machine itself which is referred to as *dulab* (wheel) or *khashab* (wood), b) the plot of land irrigated by the *dulab* and, c) the owners of the waterwheel and land. Its introduction into the area is not precisely known, but the available evidence suggests its introduction during the last millenium B.C. See W. Y. Adams, 'Continuity and Change in Nubian Cultural History' in *Sudan Notes and Records*, Vol. 48, 1967, p.15.
25 G. Kay, *Development and Underdevelopment: a Marxist Analysis*, Macmillan, 1977, p.96.
26 K. Marx, *Grundrisse: Introduction to the Critique of Political Economy*, Pelican Books, 1973, pp.256–257.
27 G. Kay, *op.cit.*, p.95
28 The term was used by E. Hobsbawm in his introduction to K. Marx's *Pre-Capitalist Economic Formations*, Lawrence and Wishart, London, 1975, p.55.

# Chapter Two: Dongola District; Geography, History and Population

## 1. Geography

The homeland of the Danagla (sing. Dongolawi, a person from Dongola District) lies along the River Nile between latitudes 18° 15′ and 19° 43′ N; and longitudes 27° 30′ and 30° 15 E in the present Northern Province of the Sudan (1974). It is the central district of the three administrative units which constitute the province: namely the Northern District, the Central District and the Southern District corresponding with the former Halfa, Dongola and Merowe Rural Councils respectively. Since 1974, these councils have been accorded District status, with a resident Assistant Provincial Commissioner, and each was divided into a number of Rural Councils – the Central District has been divided into three Rural Councils – Argo, Dongola and El Golid, and a Town Council for the town of Dongola which is the provincial capital.

The total area is about 71,277 square kilometres, (44,263 square miles) 80% of which is uncultivated desert with a population of 160,029[1] making the District sparsely populated with a density of 2.2 persons per square milometre (3.6 per square mile).[2] Its boundary in the south is at al Ghaddar and in the north at Abu Fatima near Kerma; to the east its boundary is with the Nile Province, and to the west with Northern Kordofan, Northern Darfur and Libya. These boundaries, however, do not separate the tribal groups. In the South the Bedayriyya for example, are divided between the Southern and Central Districts; and a large number of the Mahas of the Northern District are within the Central District. These boundaries are arbitrary and were made to facilitate administrative functions.

The region stands in the desert climatic zone with negligible rainfall, and the absence of nearby water surfaces made the seasons depend on the direction and speed of winds and temperature.[3] The cold dry winter, typical of desert climate, has been slightly modified by the construction of the High Dam in Egypt and the formation of Lake Nasser behind it. But the change is not sufficient to allow a change in the life of people or their animals, especially that of the formerly nomadic Arabs who settled along the river banks and in the basins of Letti and Suleim.

There are two main seasons of the year: *sayf*, summer, which extends from the beginning of May to the end of September; and *shitta*, winter, from the beginning of October to the end of April. Within this division there are two seasons which depend on the climatic conditions and mark the transitions from *sayf* to *shitta* and vice versa. One depends on the flood of the Nile, *dammiyra* and falls within the *sayf* season from July to the end of September. The other is *rabiy'*, spring, which is between *shitta* and *sayf* in March and April. These two fall within the agricultural calendar rather than the natural calendar as they do not conform to the latter divisions.

Following Barbour's classification, the District can be divided into three regions[1]:

(a) *The Eastern Desert* This is an arid zone with no rain. It is not inhabited since it can afford no living for sedentary or nomadic populations. A few *widyan* (sing. *wadi*, a water course), descend from the Red Sea Hills and these provide the only grasses found in the whole area.

(b) *The Western Desert* This area is less hostile to life, although it has most of the characteristics of the Eastern Desert. The nature of the sand there allows for some rain-water to penetrate, either from the scanty rains or from the *widyan* of Northern Kordofan. There are a few *gu'ub* (sing. *ga'ab*, oasis) where sedentary life is present with the cultivation of *dura* (sorghum vulgare), *dukhun* (millet) and some date-trees.

(c) *Nile, Suleim and Letti Basins* It is here that almost all the Danagla reside. There are continuously adjoining villages along both banks of the river above the cultivated land in the Nile basin, and a few clusters, and independent households, in the Suleim and Latti basins. Kerma and Suleim Basins are included here because they partially depend on the Nile flood though they are situated some distance away from the river course. It has also been assumed that they were probably parts of the bed of the Nile in the past.[5] They provided pasture for some Arab nomads before the digging of the irrigation canals in the first quarter of the century, and the recent introduction of perennial irrigation by means of *sagiyas* and pumps.

The Nile is traditionally the dwelling place for the Danagla. Here cultivable land was limited to what could be irrigated by the traditional *sagiya* which could not raise water beyond a narrow strip from the river. The land here is decreasing, especially on the right side of the river because of the effect of creeping sand-dunes and *haddam* (washing away of the river banks). Irrigation for this part is secured from the Nile and *matarat* (wells). The riverain area is irrigated from the Nile mainly, but Suleim and Letti basins are inundated annually during the flood season, when the silt is renewed, and irrigated from wells for the rest of the year. The Nile, then, is important for both the riverain area and the basins.

## 2. History of Settlement

The Danagla are defined with reference to the geographical area they occupy. The name Danagla (sing. Dongolawi), derives from the name of the capital of the Christian kingdom of Makurra – *Dongola al ajuz* (old Dongola). MacMichael has included the Danagla in the Ja'aliyyin group, yet his genealogical charts contain no reference to the Danagla as a tribe descending from a Ja'aliyyin ancestor.[6] Even the recent migrants of Ja'aliyyin descent do not accept that they belong to the Ja'aliyyin and claim deeper Arab ancestry. As for the earlier immigrants of Arab tribes like the Gawabra and Bidayriyya, Hassan has rejected their Ja'ali descent, '. . . Gawabra have wrongly been classified as Ja'aliyyin by MacMichael'.[7] But this does not negate the presence of some Ja'aliyyin in the area. For example, the Malik family which used to be the ruling aristocracy until recently claim ancestry from the Hakmab branch of the Ja'aliyyin.

In another place MacMichael gave a hint which supports the contention that the Danagla cannot be traced to one definite ancestry. He wrote:

> '. . . and by the fifteenth century the racial characteristics of the population in the neighbourhood of the first two cataracts, and perhaps as far south as Dongola had become substantially what they are today.'[8]

Further he wrote:

> '. . . Now as regards the Gawabra-Bidayriyya group, it is fair, I think to say that the only denomination under which they can all be classed with any accuracy is that of Danagla inhabitants, that is of Dongola, and that it is doubtful whether they were ever called Ja'aliyyin.'[9]

Crawford's statement that, 'they are Nubian in language and type', does not disregard the Danagla admixture, but he did not go into any further detail.[10] His statement refers to the original inhabitants of the area who had been successively influenced by immigrant groups of Arabs, Negroes, Egyptians and later Turks and Mamluks. The original population was 'a mixture of early Nubians and dynastic Egyptians with an ever increasing negro element.'[11] Then followed the Arabs, Egyptians, Turks and recently Arab nomads and some of the neighbouring tribes like the Mahas and the Shaiqiya.

The dominant culture is Arab, but the Danagla have retained their Nubian language. Arab descent, when claimed, suggests its pragmatic value to the consolidation of political and religious influence, or just as Hassan suggests, 'indicates a high degree of Arabisation',[12] which implies prestige within the context of the dominant Arab–Islamic culture.

For an overall understanding of the Danagla settlement two phases can be distinguished:

A. A phase when the successive immigrants were assimilated into the existing Nubian stock to form the admixture which I shall refer to as the *ahali* group hereafter. This phase roughly ends with the first Turkish occupation in 1820; and

B. A phase when the incoming groups retain their tribal identities and thus remain differentiated from the first group.

*A. Settlements before 1820*

In this phase intermingling is critical for the definition of the *ahali* group as an admixture of Nubian, Egyptian, Negroid and Arab elements. Although the Arabs attacked Nubia in 652, they were not able to penetrate further south and very few were able to settle and be assimilated, that is become Nubianized. The Arabs were checked, but in the fourteenth century they settled in large numbers to effect changes in the physical characteristics of the local population, and to a large extent, in their culture.

The Mamluks penetrated into Nubia twice; the first time in 1517 when Sultan Saleim ruled Nubia through his representative *kashifs* with a large number of Ghuzz and Bosnians as their garrisons. The second when in 1812 they fled Turkish persecution.[13] These elements settled in Nubia in sufficient numbers to modify the physical type in certain areas especially in the North. Yet some of them have preserved their physical characteristics and are treated differently from the Danagla. These are categorized, together with the recent immigrants from Egypt, as Falaliyh (sing. Fallah), a corruption of Egyptian Fellahin (peasants).

*B. Settlements after 1820*

This phase occurred with the waves of more recent immigrants who have not been assimilated into existing population. They form distinct categories which are treated as different from the earlier comers. Some have been culturally integrated into the dominant Danagla culture, yet others stand as culturally alien, like the nomadic settlers for example. I designate these groups as 'ethnic' groups as they are different, and in certain instances competing among themselves, and against the dominant *ahali* group.

After the Turkish occupation in 1820, a new system was introduced which allowed the incomers to settle as full citizens, especially in market centres, with the right to hold land. This process continued and many groups have been accommodated in the region, resulting in the present ethnic composition of the Danagla district.

Both of these categories (in A and B phases) are now referred to as Danagla as they belong to the same territorial area and speak the Dongolawi language. Outside Dongola area no other criterion is used for the definition of a Dongolawi; but within the area, there is an important differentiation, which denotes the earlier settlers (of phase A) as *ahali* that is the indigenous people; and the others defined by their respective ethnic or tribal group, for example *sudani*, which refer to ex-slaves, Falaliyh, Mahas etc.

From the foregoing classification, then, there are two categories of Danagla,[14] the *ahali* on the one hand, and other ethnic groups on the other. These ethnic categories themselves constitute different tribal groups e.g. Kababish, Hawawir, Hama Gararish for the nomadic settlers; Nuba, Fur, Dinka for the Sudaniyya; and Shawiyshiyya, Ginnawiyya, Fayyumiyya for the Falaliyh.

Ecological differences in the region influence these divisions also. In Suleim basin, where there are relatively large areas of cultivable land, the nomad settlers have gradually been assimilated in the *ahali* group. On the riverside, where the narrow strip of land had already been occupied, the nomadic settlers are separate and still retain most of their original cultural traits. They have command of the Dongolawi language, but this is not sufficient to make them *ahali*; nevertheless, they are Danagla in the broader sense of the category. The situation in the basin is not very different from that prevailing on the riverside two hundred years or so ago, when large numbers of diverse population were assimilated into the original inhabitants to form the population of today.

The processes involved in the maintenance of these divisions are competitive in nature, and the implication of this will be discussed in the respective chapters. The long history of settlement with the consequential access to the economic resources in the area, especially to land, has precipitated a situation of competition and conflicts over the economic and social resources of the region. Where land, for example, is in relative abundance, as in the Suleim basin, ethnic tensions are less, and different lines of alliances are adopted; and where land is scarce, as on the riverside, ethnic tensions are more marked.

## 3. Contemporary Ethnic Composition

In the previous section I have described the general characteristics of the Danagla. Here I will focus on the actual social groups forming the social structure of the Danagla community.

In the first Population Census of 1955/6, tribal labels were reduced thus making it difficult to classify the population ethnically and tribally. For example, the Sukkot, the Mahas and Danagla were grouped together as 'Nubians', a category which is not important for the people or for the purposes of this study. Moreover, the tribes of individuals were taken arbitrarily. Many people could relate themselves to whatever group they liked, irrespective of whether they actually belonged. This is important in itself since some like to affiliate themselves to the dominant tribal group in a particular place or village depending on their status. During an earlier study in 1974/5 in a Danagla village, Mushu, I noticed that some immigrants of Egyptian origin had been absorbed in the dominant clan in the village through a complicated system of affinal and economic relations, and eventually came to be categorized as Danagla.

In the 1955/6 Census the tribal composition of the Danagla population was given as follows:

**TABLE 1**
**1955/6 Tribal Composition of Dongola District**

| | *Tribe* | *No.* |
|---|---|---|
| 1. | Arab | 35,354 |
| 2. | Dar Hamid | 9,782 |
| 3. | Gawama 'a – Bedayriyya | 2,940 |
| 4. | Other Arab Tribes (Northern) | 9,943 |
| 5. | Ja'aliyyin | 4,930 |
| 6. | Guhayna | 7,507 |
| 7. | No Tribe | 9,907 |
| 8. | Nuba | 149 |
| 9. | Beja | 7,874 |
| 10. | Nubiyyin (Nubians) | 94,758 |
| 11. | Unknown group of Westerners | 2,063 |
| 12. | Sudanese of Egyptian Origin | 86 |
| | TOTAL | 185,293[15] |

This classification does not show the tribal composition of today, nor could it be split in any way to give a true picture of the present situation.

In 1969 a census was conducted in the Kerma-Suleim basin where the population was classified by tribe.[16] All tribes of nomadic origin were enumerated separately whereas the 1955/6 census used the 'Arab' category to include both those who resided in the basin and those who still reside in the desert. Some Danagla were thus enumerated in the categories 'Arab', 'Guhayna' and 'other Arab tribes' (Northern).

In the 1973 second Population Census, the category 'tribe' was not used but instead, a system of zoning and sectors, which is not helpful at all in the classification of people on a tribal basis. So a classification based on the 1955/6 Census will give an idea of the present ethnic composition of the Danagla. Four broad categories, namely Danagla (*ahali*), Arabs, Sudaniyya and Others (mainly Falaliyh) are used as they coincide with the people's classification and hence important in the analysis of the ethnic relations between them.

**TABLE 2**
**Classification of Population in broad ethnic categories (Based on 1955/6 Census)**

| | | |
|---|---|---|
| Danagla (ahali) | 110,502 | (3, 5, 9 and 10) |
| Arabs | 42,643 | (1, 2 and 6) |
| Sudaniyya | 2,212 | (8 and 11) |
| Others | 19,936 | (4, 7 and 12) |

In this study most of the traders fall within two of the above categories, the Danagla (*ahali*) and 'Others', which includes other Arab tribes, 'No tribe' and 'Sudanese of Egyptian Origin' in the 1955/6 Census. However, the present study reveals a number of tribal groups which were not considered as categories in the Population Census, as well as others which were lumped with other big categories like the Mahas who were counted as Nubiyyin, Nubians. I will set aside these statistical difficulties here since it is by no means possible to ascertain the numbers of each tribal or ethnic group. For the purpose of this study I am considering the most important ones which have representatives in the trading business. These are the *ahali*, mainly Danagla; Mahas; Shaiqiya; Bedayriyya; Falaliyh; Arabs which includes at least four tribal groups; and a category of 'Others' which includes Sudaniyya and Copts (who are not a tribal group but, although of Egyptian origin like the Falaliyh cannot be classified with them because of their different religion and customs).

a. *Danagla (ahali)*

This group accounts for more than a half of the total population of Dongola District. Their physical characteristics are not so different from those of the Mahas and some of the nomad settlers, but can be easily distinguished from the 'others', e.g. Sudaniyya and Falaliyh.

In 1897 they were estimated at 18,425 out of a total of 23,299 (79%),[17] and in 1955/6 they constituted 61% of the total population. In 1973, there were no figures on the official records but the comparison of two different places in the area can show the extent of their distribution. In Mushu village they form 79%[18] and in the whole Suleim basin 54%.[19]

Although their number has relatively decreased due to the influx of the nomad settlers in the area (as can be observed from the Suleim percentage) and intensive outward migration, yet they still form the dominant group in both number and influence, and are spread all over Dongola district mainly along the river banks. They are mainly cultivators but by the time that pumps were introduced for irrigation and extensive areas of land were put under cultivation, some were able to depend for a living on land rent, or on various types of investment in pump schemes, or to migrate. A defining characteristic of this group is their exclusive ownership of the riverain *milk* (freehold) land.

Political offices in the past were limited to this group. The Malik family, for example, held all political positions of the Native Administration in the Northern part (the present Argo People's Rural Council which coincides with the boundaries of their grandfathers' kingdom). The chief, deputy chief and Omdas were all from this family until that administration was abolished in 1969/70. In the southern part, deputy chiefs and Omdas were all Danagla but from different families and tribes. The tribal background for the *ahali* Danagla is not important beyond the great-grandfather and it is difficult to trace descent from any one apical ancestor. So the concept *ahali* is used for this group defined by long residence and the ownership of *milk* land.

Their economic power, which derived largely from the *milk* land ownership, was challenged by the intervention of other groups, especially the Falaliyh as traders and local entrepreneurs whose profits from trade were reinvested in *miyri* (leasehold land); this gave them access to what was once the exclusive property of the *ahali*-land. Later, education and the political and economic opportunities created by the successive governments have largely challenged the economic base of *ahali* domination; and opened the way for other groups to compete for the traditionally exclusive *ahali* values – representation for local and national political leadership.

b. *Arabs* (nomad settlers)
This group has recently become sedentary in the Kerma-Suleim and Letti Basins, and riverain areas, especially on the western bank of the river. They were formerly nomads living mostly in the western desert. They are mainly Kababish, but there are many others on the basins who are Bishariyyin, Garariysh, etc. Earlier settlers from among their tribesmen were assimilated[20] and they form a constituent element of the *ahali* group. Their settlement was forced on them during the last thirty years. After a series of droughts in the Western desert many came with their animals and settled on the outskirts of the riverain villages. Gradually they started to lose their animals and many turned to agriculture as an occupation, beginning as casual agricultural labourers at harvest seasons and later becoming permanent tenants. The stagnant land situation, which was not amenable to extension under the technical conditions of the time, did not allow the assimilation of these nomadic settlers like their predecessors. So the newly opened land in the basins (especially the Suleim after 1969 and the Burgeig Government Scheme), and also the *miyri* land behind the villages, drew a large number of the nomads as share-croppers and tenants. At present the basins are their places of concentration (they form 24% of the total population on the Suleim basin[21]) and they are fairly well represented in almost all riverain villages, where they have separate residential quarters. The redistribution of the Suleim basin land in 1969/70 gave them an opportunity to hold land. The slogan 'Land for the tiller' was implemented in the first year of the present government. A limited land reform was introduced, aiming at the appropriation of the *miyri* land by those who actually undertake cultivation. Most of the share-croppers were given land that they had worked for their landlords.[22] This was advantageous for the share-croppers and agricultural labourers on the lands of big landlords like the former Shaykhs and Omdas. An example of the extent of the expropriation was an Omda who held 82 tenancies of 820 faddans, 750 faddans of which were given to his tenants.

Their role in political life was insignificant, especially those who were living within the riverain villages. Until recently, they felt that they were guests of their *ahali* hosts and as such excluded from important matters concerning the villages as a whole. Since the coming to power of the new regime in 1969, they have been gradually gaining political influence as well as economic strength in the area. Under the political situation of universal suffrage and equal opportunities, the *ahali* are becoming very anxious about the presence of nomad settlers in their villages. Before then, they were excluded from taking an active role in village politics, yet their mobilization at the national political level was an activity which certain political parties in the past benefited from. In Dongola district, there is a tendency for the villagers to demand separate institutions for the nomad settlers. Three of the village councils are already facing such problems, which pose many difficulties for the administrators and politicians alike. The nomad settlers, on the other hand, are demanding the same as they are usually not fully represented. From the villagers' side, some do not want their traditional political influence in village affairs to be endangered by the interests of the new settlers. On the other hand, the settlers do have their own grievances as they think that they are not given the say in the affairs of the villages to which they are officially entitled.

Moreover, the nomads are not given their due share of rationed goods, the administration of which has for the last five years been the major task of the village councils. Nevertheless, alliances based on different common interests are not absent from the relationships between some sections of the *ahali* and the nomad settlers. A case from Kaptode village, north of Dongola town, can throw some light on the type of alliances which can be formed in the area.

The village council of Kaptode had ten members (in 1977) from the village *ahali* and nine from the Deim el Ababda nomad settlement above the village. This settlement is situated on the camp site of the Mahdist forces, and has been there since 1898 within the boundaries of the village. The fathers and grandfathers of these Ababda played an important role in the Mahdiyya, both as fighters and despatch riders. They are all *ansar*, followers of the Mahdi, and as such were supporters of the now banned Umma party. The Ababda members of the village council allied themselves with the *ansar* among the *ahali* in the village, and these are reluctant to participate in the new institutions created by the Government like the Sudanese Socialist Union (SSU), the village councils, Development Committees etc. The supporters of the government in the council, who are mostly drawn from the local SSU Basic Unit, were anxious to show their allegiance to the party and the Provincial authorities. Failing to defeat the *ansar* alliance (village and settlement members), the SSU members applied to the province authorities to separate the settlers from the village council, claiming that they were independent and different, geographically separated and with different interests from those of the villagers. The fact of being allied with the 'rightist' and 'revisionist' elements in the village was included in the SSU Basic Unit application.[23] An investigation was carried out by the provincial authorities, and two separate councils for the village and the settlement were eventually established. But some of the Ababda (Rakhayab) are still within the geographical boundaries of the village (C in the sketch below). The SSU members are still (1977) trying to separate these which threaten the

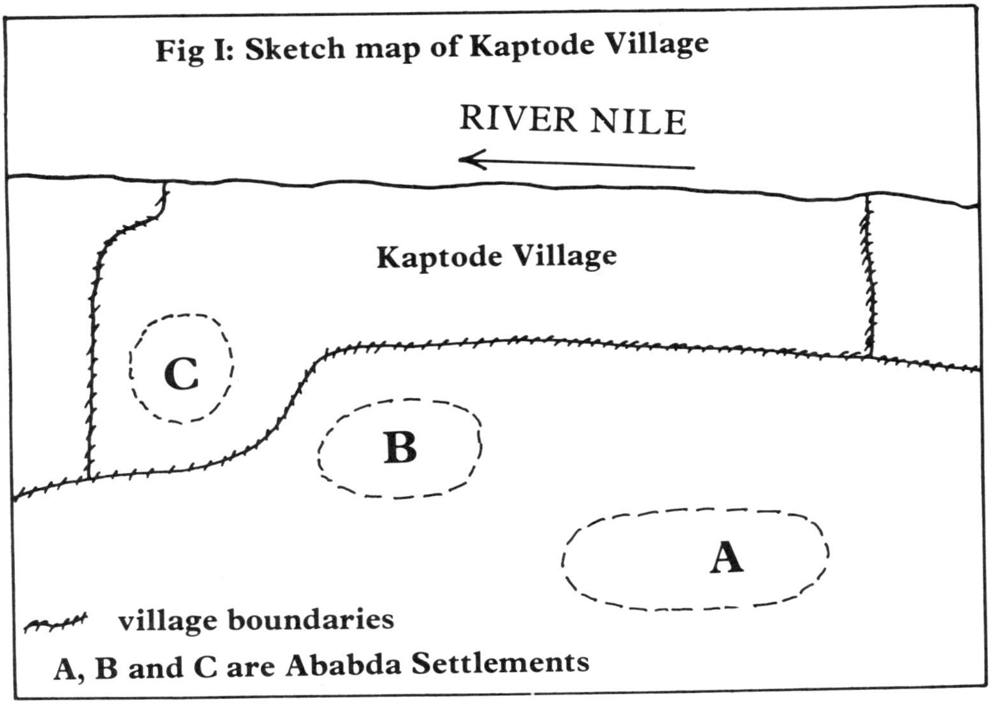

*ahali* access to the *miyri* land above the village and also constitute a continuous threat of their future alliances with the *ansar* of the village. The fact that the village would lose access to extensions in the hinterland was used by the *ansar ahali* in their campaign to dominate the newly formed council; and it proved to be appealing to the village voters, who supported them. Yet until the time I left the area (June 1977), the two councils were classified as the most inactive councils in the Central District,[24] because of the continuing disputes which brought the village councils to a standstill.

This case shows how the settling nomads are still leading an ambivalent political life; on the one hand they are fully-fledged citizens with equal political and civic rights deriving from the fact of domicile, while on the other hand the villagers look on these settlers as alien groups who set their social and political relations in a state of imbalance. Also it shows how national policies can sometimes be incompatible with local situations and needs. The position of the village SSU is contradictory to the declared policy of the party, which calls for broadly defined concepts of citizenship and equal rights. At the same time the local SSU leaders declared war against 'rightist' and 'revisionist' elements in the village. Their conflict against the *ansar* of the village was thus extended to the nomad settlers who, being deprived of many rights in the past, do expect the SSU to be helpful rather than hostile, according to the declared policy of the party.

Such a situation is not sufficient to drive the nomad settlers back to their former environment since the economic advantages in staying where they are now, greatly outbalance any possibility of return, especially if we take into consideration the change in the climate and the long severance from their nomadic way of life. Moreover, the experience of sedentary life for a prolonged time has developed ideas and aspirations different from their old ones. They are now building permanent houses, holding land, and adopting sedentary agriculture as a mode of economic life.

c. *Sudaniyya*

This group comprises the formerly negro slaves *'abiyd*, and most of the recent comers from the western and southern parts of the Sudan. They have dark colour and clearly negroid features, and are easily distinguished from other groups. Their number has been continuously decreasing.[25] Under the *sagiya* system of cultivation they provided the labour needed for hazardous agricultural and domestic tasks. Later, in the 1920's[26], slavery was made illegal and many of them left for other parts of the Sudan, especially towns, in order to change locality and to evade the stigma of slave ancestry. Those who remained behind are those who retain close ties with their ex-masters, or who were forcibly turned back from Karima town while on their way to other towns. The colonial government, though it enacted the laws forbidding slavery, was threatened by a drop in food-crop production after many slaves had moved out. As a precaution many were prevented from taking trains southward.[27]

However, for those who stayed, the freedom given was insufficient in a community where land is the main source of livelihood, and since they were not in a position to own land, they continued as dependents with their former masters as share-croppers and agricultural labourers, an occupation which until now they have been sharing with the nomad settlers along the river.

Culturally, they are the nearest to the *ahali* group because of their long association and interaction. They speak the Nubian language fluently as well as having most of their traditions and customs. Generally they were the second ethnic group to settle and be assimilated into Danagla culture, but as social inferiors.

d. *Falaliyh*

This is a category used for Sudanese of Turkish or Mamluk origin. The history of their settlement has been described earlier in this chapter. Most of them were counted under the categories of 'No tribe' and 'Sudanese of Egyptian origin' in the 1955/6 Population Census (see p.00). No exact figure can be given, but they form a significant minority of Dongola District population. In the traders' questionnaire undertaken for this study, they formed 13.4% of the retailers and 64.7% of the wholesalers in the area showing their economic importance in spite of their being a minority. They dominate the external trade and constitute a sizeable proportion of the retail trade, especially in their towns of concentration, Dongola and Argo. Most of the Falaliyh or their fathers returned to the area with the army of occupation in 1898. They had lived in the area before the Mahdiyya but in 1884 fled back to Southern Egypt for fear of persecution by the Mahdist armies. Some stayed, but they were very few compared to the *muhajiriyn* (emigrants), who came back with the advancing army and provided some services to it. Some having previous knowledge about the area were of high value for the army intelligence services; this helped them in establishing themselves at first as craftsmen and later as traders.

Until 1916 they were referred to in the official documents and land transactions and registration as Egyptians. After 1916 they were referred to as *mawaliyd* (born here) until 1956 when the category tribe was dropped from many registration forms. Since then they have been classified as Sudanese without reference to tribe for formal purposes, although the categories Danagla, Mahas and Shaiqiya are still in use.

Internally the Falaliyh are highly differentiated and have at least twelve different lineages and the pattern developing of such differentiation can allow for the formation of more lineages. Unlike those of the *ahali* or nomadic settlers these lineages are only two or three generations deep, and it is only through inter-marriage that any kinship relation can be found between these different and independent units. The name of the lineage derived from the founding father, who usually arrived by himself at the end of the last century. If the father had had a distinguished occupation, the lineage then is defined by that occupation. For example, the Kayyaliyn are descendents of a *kayyal*, a grain seller; this is not his actual name. Some are known by the places in Egypt from which the father migrated, e.g. Ginnawiyya, coming from Ginna in Upper Egypt. Others are named after the father's job by using the adjectival form of the job name. Most of these seemed to have good employment positions with the government administration, police or the army like Shawiyshiyya, those descendents of a *shawiysh*, a sergeant; Affendiyya, those of an *affendi*, a titled used for clerks and junior administrators by the Turks and the colonial government later.

Now they are entering different occupations, especially the young generation who work as teachers, clerks etc.; but the most important occupation for them is trade and related businesses like butcheries, bakeries, flour mills, etc. Some are engaged in agriculture, especially those in the Suleim basin.

e. *Others*

Here smaller tribal groups are briefly described including the Mahas, Shaiqiya, Bedayriyya, Copts and Others.

*Mahas* Apart from a very few Mahas traders in the northern part (60 retailers and two wholesalers) most are concentrated in the Suleim basin and Burgeig scheme as tenants. When the Burgeig scheme was established in 1944, the *ahali* were reluctant to move to it from their riverside villages. The government, then, brought in some Egyptian fellahin, Mahas, Shaiqiya and Manasiyr to help with the production of wheat and other cereals in the scheme.[28] Dongola with a comparatively larger area of cultivable land than the Mahas homeland, the Belly of Stones, was a relief for the population pressure there. Those who could not migrate outside the province for wage employment, were able to find sufficient land to cultivate in the Suleim and Burgeig schemes.

*Shaiqiya* They are very few and are concentrated in the Burgeig scheme in particular.[29] They do not speak the Danagla language and still maintain relations with their homeland in the Southern district. Occupationally they are mainly tenants in the Burgeig and Suleim and a few are traders in the towns of Argo and Kerma. They are considered to be outsiders by the Danagla, and because of the nature of their ties with the homeland, they are more migrant settlers than a resident group.

*Copts* These are not different from the Falaliyh in their physical characteristics. Originally they came from Egypt after the Re-Occupation as traders. They are few in numbers now as they have experienced great movement from the area into Khartoum and Omdurman. Being of different religion from that of the Danagla may account for their separation and aloofness. Nevertheless, one of them has achieved the highest economic and political position possible in his village. Noon, of El Golid, a trader and farmer, is the chairman of almost all the political and welfare organizations in the village and the president of the rural council. But the few other families (there are only seven altogether in the whole Central District) are not involved in such activities and concentrate their efforts in trade.

*Bidayriyya* These are mainly in the southern part of the district with their concentration in the Southern District. They are mostly sedentary cultivators and not different from the *ahali* and Shaiqiya in either their physical characteristics or way of life, but are monolingual like the Shaiqiya. They speak Arabic only.

*Khanadga* These are the residents of Khandag, which was an important junction of trade routes to Egypt in the past. They claim that they are originally Egyptians. Their forefathers were traders between Egypt and Sudan and at a certain time they settled as agents for the collection of goods for their Egyptian clients. Since then they have been maintaining a different way of life and despite their long settlement (about 200 years) they do not understand or speak the Danagla language. Their village is devoid of agricultural land except for one island which provides them with fodder for their domestic animals. They depend totally on migration and the Khanadga traders are well known all over the Sudan. Their economic prosperity from a long trading experience furnished them with the necessary wealth to educate their children, most of whom are assuming high positions in the government offices.

There are other tribal groups which neither are important for the study nor have any influence in the life of the Danagla community. Most of them are casual visitors and their stay in the area is very short, like the Fallata who are hawkers around the villages selling perfumes, beads and peanuts; and the Halab (gypsies) who are also itinerant blacksmiths and china-ware traders.

The population composition described above shows a clear pattern of distribution of the ethnic groups in the region. The availability of economic resources especially land

and irrigation water played an important role not only in distribution but also in the relationships between the different ethnic groups constituting the Danagla community. These ecological factors have been important in determining the pattern of earlier and recent settlements. The nomads, for example, were forced to settle in certain places like the Suleim basin while their settlement in the villages has largely been constrained by the land situation there. We cannot, therefore, expect nomad settlers in islands nor can we find any Mahas in the southern part. The only groups that are fairly represented all over the region are the *ahali*, the Sudaniyya, and to a lesser extent the Falaliyh whose concentration is mostly in the towns and the northern part. However, the relationships between the different groups constitute the basis of the Danagla social structure and can be used as indicators of the impact of the socio-economic development taking place in the area as that reflects clearly on these relations.

## Notes

1 *1973 Population Census of the Sudan*, Provincial Office of Statistics, Dongola.
2 Prospective cultivable land is about 250,000 *faddans*. *Annual Report 1976/77, Assistant Commissioner for Agricultural Affairs, Dongola.*
3 *See K. M. Barbour, The Republic of the Sudan*, University of London Press, 1964, p.138.
4 *ibid.*, p.138.
5 *ibid.*, p.132.
6 See H. A. MacMichael, *A History of the Arabs in the Sudan*, London, 1922, p.222.
7 Yusuf Fadl Hassan, *The Arabs and the Sudan*, University of Khartoum Press, 1973, Note 50, p.250.
8 H. A. MacMichael, *op. cit.*, p.198.
9 *ibid.*, p.198.
10 O. G. S. Crawford, *The Fung Kingdom of Sennar*, Gloucester, 1951.
11 Seligman, quoted by MacMichael, *op. cit.*, p.15.
12 See Y. F. Hassan, *op. cit.*, p.135.
13 A. J. Arkell 'Dongola', in *Encyclopaedia Britannica*, Vol. 7, 1961.
14 From now onwards the word 'Danagla' refers to all residents of Dongola District and the term *ahali* will be used exclusively to the indigenous settlers of phase 'A' of my classification.
15 This total shows a difference between the tribal distribution and the total number given for the area which was 151,736.
16 See Tag el Sir Abdul Mutalib, *Socio-Economic Survey of the Kerma-Suleim basin*, Ministry of Agriculture, Khartoum, 1970.
17 *Intelligence Report, Egypt, January 1897*, Sudan Collection, University of Khartoum Library.
18 A village census conducted by the writer in 1974.
19 See Abdul Mutalib, *op. cit.*, p.32.
20 See H. A. MacMichael, *op. cit.*, p.198.
21 See Abdul Mutalib, *op. cit.*, p.32.
22 This was accompanied by problems for the former share-cropping tenants over compensating fixed assets of the landlords, and by illicit agreements which allowed for the former landlords to regain influence over most of the present tenants. For more details see section IV chapter V.
23 A memorandum to the Commissioner and Secretary of the SSU, Dongola, File entitled *Village Councils*, Dongola People's Rural Council.
24 *ibid.*
25 In 1897 they were 2,548 forming about 11% of the then Danagla population. *Intelligence Report, Egypt, January 1897.* In 1955/6 they were 2,212, that is about 1.6% of the population. See *First Population Census of the Sudan 1955/6*. Department of Statistics, Khartoum.

26 Although among the first legislation after the Re-Conquest in 1898 was the abolition of slave trade, yet it was not until the twenties that action was taken to stop domestic slavery and to free the existing slaves.

27 See Al-Shahi, A. S., *An Anthropological Study of a Northern Sudan Shaiqiya Village*, Unpublished Ph.D. Thesis, Oxford, 1971, pp.132–3.

28 See the Burgeig scheme, p. 72.

29 Eight families from one village in a Shaiqiya village were reported to live on the Burgeig scheme. It is clear that a relative who is in Burgeig can arrange for other relatives to join. See *Al-Shahi, op. cit.*, 111-112.

# Chapter Three: The Kinship System

## The Kinship System and Marriage Patterns

In this region it is difficult to write about a kinship system which embraces the whole population of Dongola District, but an attempt is made here to describe the dominant pattern, that is of the numerically dominant *ahali* group. However, the kinship organization of other groups is described in the appropriate places where they reveal a significant difference. For the purpose of this study, the kinship organization under the *sagiya* system of production is taken as the starting point of analysis because it is difficult to obtain information about earlier forms, and because there are at present some elderly people who themselves had been a part of that system. Under the *sagiya*, the local agnatic group consisting of small lineages of three to four generations constituted the basis of social organization, and within that group the extended family and the joint family were important in the economic organization of the villages and represented production as well as consumption units. As I will show, the kinship relations were generally, and still are, limited to a very narrow sphere of interaction in village or inter-village relations. They are important mainly for moral support and in reciprocal exchanges in matters concerning life crises such as marriage, death, circumcision ceremonies, etc., which are the domain of the agnatic descent groups; though they are sometimes also mobilized for economic and political support in the village political and economic activities.

## The Structure of the ahali-descent-group

What is defined as a descent group here is a group of people who are patrilineally related, who own one *sagiya* or more jointly, and who can trace their descent from the first owner of the plot of land they hold. Strangers could also acquire membership of the group, mainly through marriage. But in such a situation we find that one becomes incorporated in the original *sagiya*-owning group if one is to live permanently with that group. The group, then, has ways of recruiting new members: it gives its women in marriage to outsiders or newcomers of relatively high status; or it gets rid of women who may be insane or promiscuous, in which case the status of the husband is unimportant. In the past people of religious knowledge who came as teachers of the Koran could acquire land and marry from the local groups, and being highly regarded for their piety, might start a new lineage in the village with its own *sagiya*, the land for it being originally taken from that of other groups in the form of gifts in return for their services, or in recognition of their piety – an exceptional quality which lessens the force of queries about origin and descent. Also people of authority could be incorporated, like former officers of the Turkish and Egyptian armies. Through long association they were able to acquire land by purchase or through marriage into weaker descent groups in the villages. An example is that of an Egyptian who settled in the village of Mushu as a vegetable cultivator, attaching himself to a village magnate as a share-cropper. By and by the patron gave him his daughter in marriage together with a gift of land which came to exceed the nominal *sagiya* size at the time of registration in 1907, and since then there has been a *sagiya* in his name, which is enough to attribute to him *ahali* group membership. His descendants, *Wilad ab Shanab*, are fully incorporated in the wider category of *ahali* and the descent group organization so that his Egyptian origin is no longer referred to. As time goes on this type of recruitment to, and splitting off from, descent groups is no longer taking place because of the stagnant situation on the *milk* land, which forms the basis of recruitment and identification. In the past there was enough *milk* land to provide for strangers and outsiders who could be assimilated. Land is getting scarcer and has become of greater social significance as a defining characteristic of the *ahali* group, the highest of the social groups constituting the Danagla community. At the present there is no way of incorporating strangers since access to *milk* land is blocked by descent group endogamy, and by ethnic group endogamy, which makes acquisition of *milk* land practically impossible; and hence attention has been directed to *miyri* land, and the role of marriage in gaining access to land and other social resources has been reduced.

**Marriage and the descent group**

The changes which have influenced the structure of the descent groups have also precipitated important changes in the system of marriage. Under the *sagiya* system of production,[1] the ideal marriage was within the agnatic descent group which owned the *sagiya*; within the extended family, which might totally or partially own a *sagiya* with other members of the agnatic group; or with any woman who could be classified as *bint 'am*, paternal parallel cousin. Contrary to the pattern within the *ahali* group, the *falaliyh* pattern appears to be more dogmatic about the 'within-the-family' marriages.[2] This situation is comparable to that of the *ahali* under the *sagiya* system which is now giving way to different values in the selection of spouses. The traditionally preferred marriage, between paternal parallel cousins, was dependent on the organization of the extended families as one unit to cope with the mode of production centred around the *sagiya* as a joint property on which the extended family worked corporately. The preservation of the property and the stability of the kinship group necessitated marriage with the father's brother's daughter as a means of keeping the family and its property intact, as inheritance mainly follows the patriline. Failing this ideal marriage, any classifactory patrilineal cousin would do. So although this marriage was the ideal, yet it provided for more preferential marriages within the agnatic group and occasionally outside it. We find a system, then, where cultural values work strongly to emphasize the importance of parallel cousin marriage though in practice it formed only a fraction of the marriages contracted. W. and A. Kronenberg have described a similar situation for the northern Nubians which could also explain the discrepancies in the ideal and actual marriages among the Danagla. They arrived at the conclusion that the kinship system and cultural values '. . . are focused on the marriage of parallel cousins to such an extent that every marriage may ultimately be regarded as a marriage between parallel cousins'.[3]

In my study of Mushu village I found that although the villagers, especially among the *ahali* group, stress that their marriages are within the family circle, it appeared on close interview that very few of the spouses had actually married the father's brother's daughters. Among the older generations (more than 45 years), it was found that 13.7 per cent of the total number of heads of households in the village actually married their father's brother's daughters (47 out of 343), while 56.5 per cent married from non-relatives (194 out of 343). The figures for married children of these heads of households show a movement away from the ideal marriage, as only 4.8 per cent (4 out of 83) married their actual father's brother's daughter. The marriage of non-relatives has not changed much as still 60 per cent (50 out of 83) married into the category 'non-relatives' as compared to that of the older generation (56.5 per cent).[4] From these figures we can see that even in the past the Danagla were not strictly following the patrilineal parallel cousin marriage but it occurred statistically more than it does now; this illustrates how the mode of social and economic organization under the *sagiya* was more restrictive on marriage alliances within the village. This may suggest a preference for the selection of spouses from the residual category of relatives, where most women can be classified as *banat 'am*. As the village figures show, 30 per cent of the men in the older generation married from the category 'relative'. This is matched by a slightly different percentage of the younger generation (35 per cent). The two percentages show a slight difference between the two generations as regards marriage with relatives; and when we add the percentages of the parallel cousin marriages these make 44 per cent and 40 per cent for the older generation and their children respectively. We can derive from these figures that marriages are concluded mainly with outsiders, that is outside the agnatic descent group, and were so, in the past, although many occurred within the circle of relatives; this includes maternal relatives, with the bias towards the paternal relatives.

As for the residential arrangements, the Danagla used to build their houses within the boundaries of their *sagiyas* so that women on marriage move into the *sagiya* to the husband's house; or, as often was the case, they were already within the *sagiya* of the husband. Sons bring their wives to the father's households where they build bedrooms within the courtyard of the father. Apart from the bedrooms, the house is shared by all the members of the family with a bigger front room, *diywan*, to entertain guests and visitors.

With the decreasing areas in the *milk* land to house the ever-increasing population, and with the growing importance of *milk* land for growing date trees, the Danagla tend to build their houses in the *miyri* land – a tendency which has always been encouraged by the local authorities so that better use of the fertile *sagiya* land could be made. This development has influenced the pattern of residence not only as concerns the agnatic descent group clusters themselves, but also in terms of the heterogeneity of the new residential areas as a result of the convergence of different descent groups and the presence of members of non-*ahali* ethnic groups. With the other external influences, like the relative independence of children who emigrate and have wage employment outside, which furnishes them with the costs of building their separate houses, we find that post-marriage residence is moving from one which was characteristically patrilocal to one which is increasingly neolocal, a development that adds to the weakening of the corporateness of the extended family which started when its role as a production unit diminished, and finished with the ending of its role as a consumption unit too. It is evident that patrilocal residence as well as preferential parallel cousin marriage have experienced changes which are connected in various ways with the decline in the importance of the extended family, and to a lesser extent of the agnatic descent group, as bases for economic and social organization. This in turn can be related to changes in the system of production (which will be analysed when we discuss the *sagiya* system of production and its transformation) together with the comparatively slow changes at the superstructural level.

The foregoing description applies mainly to the *ahali* group; as it is the dominant group, at least numerically, their kinship system depicts the dominant form of kinship organization among the Danagla. There are other forms of kinship organization in the region, within the different constituent ethnic groups. The nomadic settlers, for example, still maintain some relationships with their relatives in the desert and in different parts of the region. When they came to settle on the outskirts of the villages their settlement was usually in small numbers of relatives, depending on the employment opportunities the village offered. As I have shown in Chapter Two, their settlement was temporary at first, as they came to the villages during the harvest seasons, which offered both work for them and fodder for their animals. At the end of the harvest season they retreated to their settlements in the desert to join their kinsmen. When they gradually started to lose their herds as a result of drought, they began settling permanently on the outskirts of villages with their remaining animals. Their pattern of settlement was then influenced by their work relations prior to permanent settlement. In almost all the villages, most of the settlers are either brothers, or fathers and children or, in larger settlements, they are a whole section of a lineage of the nomadic tribe. I am not going to describe the different kinship systems of the nomadic settlers because they vary from tribe to tribe and because they are not important for the understanding of settler relationships with the rest of the Danagla in the economic and political spheres. Their kinship systems continue to have a bearing on their marriages, as they cannot intermarry with the *ahali*; and consequently they marry within their own lineages or into others in the same tribal groups.

The Sudaniyya, who are mainly the ex-slaves (or their descendants) of the *ahali* group, do not differ noticeably from the pattern of the *ahali*. After the Re-occupation slavery was legally abolished and this allowed the male slaves, who were more mobile, to leave the area for better chances outside. Hence there has been a discrepancy in their sex-ratio with a large number of women slaves left behind. These women became dependent on their masters for economic and moral support. This dependency extended to the control over their sexuality as the masters chose who they would give them to in marriage, taking into consideration factors which would not matter in *ahali* marriages. The most important factor is the perpetuation of this dependency and the guarantee of continuous domestic assistance needed by the masters' womenfolk. In the study of Mushu village the figures suggest a tendency for marriage with mother's brother's or mother's sister's daughter. This would ensure that the marriage was concluded among the slaves of the ex-master and, with the immobility of women would safeguard the continuous loyalty of a family slave group, which, though its economic role has changed, still renders certain services for the families that once owned it, especially on occasions when manual work is needed like chopping wood or carrying water in ceremonials.

**The extended family and the** ***sagiya***

The wider kinship unit, that is the local descent group, comes together for corporate action on the occasions referred to earlier, but where we find the manifestation of corporateness is in the production of subsistence crops where the extended or joint family own and work together in the *sagiya*. The *sagiya* was a production and sometimes a consumption unit as well. It consisted of people who defined their relations with others as either *ahl* (relatives who are neighbours), interacted with the others accordingly, and referred to themselves as a *sagia of X*; or in certain contexts they called themselves *nas* X (i.e. X's people or clan), which refers to the one in whose name the *sagiya* land was initially registered, or the senior member of the living owners of the *sagiya*.

The smallest residential unit, *heiy* (quarter) was made up of different descent groups in the past when it was built on *milk* land; now that *miyri* land has started to be used for housing, it is made up of different ethnic groups. We may find a dominant clan within one or in most of the quarters of the village. When the *milk* land was the only residential area houses were built within the agnatic descent group property (the *sagiya*), on the higher parts of the land which were normally on the side away from the river. So owners of different *sagiyas* may form intermittent clusters which have collective names despite their internal differentiation into separate *sagiyas* and descent groups. Such clusters do not derive their names from the descent groups except where a group owns a number of *sagiyas* and is larger than the normal four or five nuclear families living jointly. These clusters derive their names from a physical characteristic or a feature such as a clump of trees, or an event such as a natural disaster.

Although the extended family, which constituted the household with shared arrangements under the *sagiya* system, was the only unit within these clusters that acted corporately in economic matters, yet the clusters have relations of mutual help in tasks like house repairs, or preparation and cooking a feast among womenfolk. On the higher level of the village, relationships are mostly confined to reciprocation in matters concerning life crises and other social occasions, where the relationships deriving from neighbourliness and village co-residence are reinforced by financial transactions, *gaddah*, whereby people advance money or goods to help with the costs, in the expectation of reciprocity. These relations still exist but not only is co-operation in the production process decreasing for the clusters and the descent groups comprising them, but also the decline is noted in the corporateness and solidarity of the extended family, which has gradually given way to a nuclear family organization.

The fact that the organization of economic production defines, in many respects, the kinship system and the internal organization of the peasant families is an important proposition of this study. It has been observed in the Danagla situation that where individual effort has been increasingly substituted for the communal descent-group one, this has been accompanied by the decline of the extended family's importance. The introduction of capital-intensive agricultural machinery allows the individual either to invest directly in installing a pump, which needs the accumulation of capital, or else to work as a tenant or share-cropper in the *sagiyas* and later in the pump schemes established by individuals or partnerships. The peasant here, faces these schemes as an individual willing to cultivate and ready to share his produce with the scheme owners in exchange for irrigational water; this is unlike his situation under the *sagiya*, when he shared the ownership of both land and the means of irrigation. He is no longer dependent on the family group to obtain the land on which he expends his labour, nor is he capable of getting the collaboration of the extended family for co-operation. He has more freedom to join any of the schemes in the vicinity and hence the loss of identification with a particular *sagiya* both as a production and as a social unit.[5] He needs the help of the immediate nuclear family of wife and children to assist with some agricultural activities in his tenancy, but for the activities that need many hands, harvesting for example, he draws help from the co-tenants in the scheme irrespective of any local or kinship relationship.[6] The extended family, however, has now been minimized in production, whereas in small pumps (3″ to 5″ sucking calibre) the kinship ties still retain some importance. This is because many of the small pumps were installed in the place of *sagiyas* not in order to expand production (that is clear from the limitations on the *milk* land), but merely to replace the *sagiya* and reproduce its organization. The land cultivated is still *milk* and the types of crops grown still those which were characteristically suitable for small areas such as date trees, lucerne and vegetables. The installation of these small pumps, except for those installed by traders in the first phases of their agricultural investments, has been largely accomplished by the members of the extended families owning the *milk* land with the help of their savings and the remittances sent from outside by the migrant members of the *sagiya* owners, but this type of family investment is limited in its social and economic consequences for the village, or the whole community.

The process of nuclearization of the extended family referred to above has resulted mainly from the extensive agriculture developed after the introduction of large schemes and the integration of the local economy with a wider market economy by the activities of local and national entrepreneurs. The substantial private investment in agriculture has influenced the family economic role and gradually influenced its structure. For the community as a whole, the Danagla are very conscious of their ethnic identity, their consanguineal bonds and, to a lesser extent, their kin endogamy, yet these are mostly subservient to other considerations of an economic and political nature especially if we look into the relationships in the villages or for the region as a whole.

Competition for the ownership of *miyri* land and holding of political positions are becoming primary in the formation of political alliances within the villages, and in this are taking the place of the weakening kinship ties which are becoming more localized and limited to personal and familial matters. There follow then two different situations: in the first we have the descent groups consisting of extended families residing in one locality and working corporately to provide the necessary labour under the *sagiya* system as well as political and moral support; and in the other where the corporate character has changed in a relatively short time, the members of the groups are separated from their means of production and stand as individuals instead. Moreover these individuals are put in this situation with new requirements of agricultural production within new forms of organization, techniques and relations of production.

## Notes

1 See Chapter Five for details of the *sagiya* organization.
2 The reasons for *falaliyh* endogamy seem to stem from the fact that they are a minority with distinctive physical and cultural characteristics. Their monopoly of the big trading businesses may partially explain their endogamy not only as an ethnic group but also within the constituent lineages of this group. Hence intermarriage is possible with wealthy *ahali* or their chiefs.
3 See A. and W. Kronenberg, 'Parallel Cousin Marriage in Medieval and Modern Nubia, Part II', in *Kush*, Vol. 13, 1965.
4 Figures are from a village census conducted by the writer for Mushu village in February–May 1974.
5 This does not mean the loss of land in the *sagiya*.
6 See Section II, Chapter Four.

# Chapter Four: Factors of Production: Land, Capital and Labour

In Dongola, as is generally the case in riverain areas of the Northern Sudan, agricultural production has largely been constrained by the availability of capital for investment in the provision of irrigation. In an area where rain is negligible the importance of irrigation is as great as the availability of land. Here I will describe the economic resources in the area, viz. land, capital and labour, as they provide an indispensable background to understanding the development of the existing production relations. However, the description of the different forms of capital accumulation will be very brief here as this will be described elsewhere.[1] The purpose here is to show the relationship between these resources and how they have been influenced by different factors of change both from within and from outside and the consequent influences on the relations of production in agriculture.

**Section I Land Types and Control**

Although I have stressed the importance of capital as the main constraint on agricultural investment, yet land, as an object of this investment, has played its role in constraining for a long time those who had the money to invest until the character of land was changed, or the involvement of the investors changed from one type of land to another.

Land is of two types in respect of its legal position, the one registered as freehold, *milk*; and the other registered as leasehold from the government, *miyri*. Each of these has different sub-types defined by location, means of irrigation or production potential.[2] These two main categories (*milk* and *miyri*) will be described with regard to their characteristics, their use and means of acquisition. Both of the two types have different attributes deriving from their ownership or control. Outright ownership is

**Figure II: A cross-section showing land types in Dongola Area**

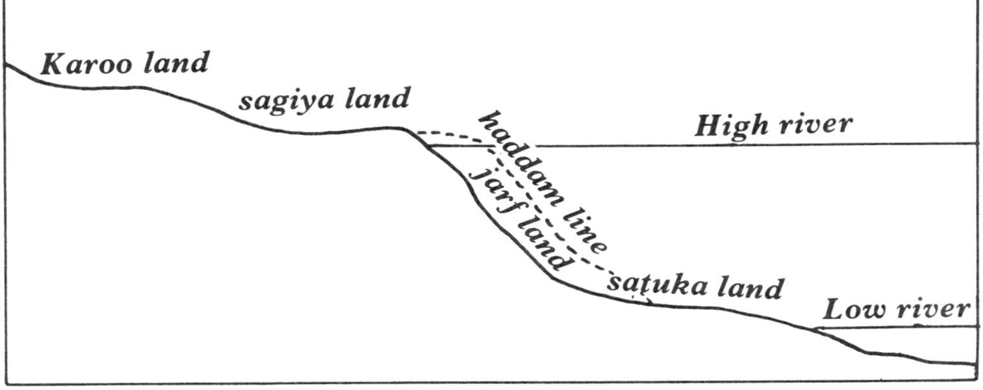

only in the *milk* land but control and utilization have become of great importance in the *miyri* land. This development has removed land-holding from being an attribute defining other ethnic groups in relation to the dominant *ahali* group, to a factor which influences the changes which have been taking place in the Danagla social structure.

*Milk Land* In 1899, the condominium government of the Sudan issued its first rules of land registration allowing land which was continuously possessed in the previous five years to be an absolute title of the holder.[3] These rules were faced with many difficulties as the land was individually held and its possession was customarily recognized without the complexities of registration. The rules followed a period when the Danagla experienced one of their great migrations to Central and Western Sudan as a result of the excessive Turkish taxes. The Turkish authorities used to sell the land of those who were not able to pay. What made the situation worse was the inability of some returnees (in the Mahdiyya) to retrieve their lands, and they had either to stay landless or migrate to other parts of the Sudan, especially after the Re-Conquest of the country in 1899.[4] Consequently a considerable number of the *ahali* group became landless.[5] Ever since then, *milk* land has been, not only economically valuable, but a prestigious asset, and hence protected from any intrusion by strangers or relatives who were dispossessed. A complicated land-tenure system developed which will be described in relation to the development of different share-cropping arrangements in the region (Chapter 5).

The area of *milk* land is finite and more susceptible to decrease by river washing (*haddam*. See Plate 1). Also we find that rights of heredity, based on Islamic rules but modified by local practices, subjected this type of land to excessive fragmentation; hence the plots do not form any economically viable units for crop production. The following example taken from the Land Register of Dongola District will illustrate the extent of fragmentation:

> *sagiya* number 18, Agada registered in 1909 under the name Osman Khayri with an area of 11 *feddans* and 481 square metres.
>
> In 1933 Osman Khayri died and his land was divided among his heirs, and each given the following shares:
>
> Two wives given 0.46 faddan each (1,945 sq.m.)
> Three sons given 1.75 faddan each (7,374 sq.m.)
> Five daughters given 0.89 each (3,727 sq.m.)
> One of the sons was given 81 sq.m. by consent of the rest.
>
> In 1966 his elder son died and his share (1.75 faddans) was divided among his wife, two sons and four daughters.
> His wife received 0.21 faddans (891 sq.m.)
> Two sons each one received 0.38 faddan (1,620 sq.m.)
> Four daughters each one received 0.19 faddans (810 sq.m.).[6]

Attempts by the government to amalgamate these scattered small units failed and since then the government has directed its attention to the *miyri* land for agricultural development.[7] The only government pumping scheme in the region, the Burgeig, for example, was wholly established on *miyri* land in order to avoid the difficulties inherent in the milk land, especially those of fragmentation and the attachment of the people to land in ways which are not favourable to rational production.

The *sagiya* is the most important type of *milk* land. It extends as a narrow strip along the river banks and used to be the only land that could be irrigated by the *sagiya*, from which it has derived its name.[8] Acquisition of such land, apart from inheritance, proved to be difficult though not impossible as there have been instances of transfer through purchase and gifts within the land-owning kinship groups. There are four ways of acquiring *milk* land; chief among them is inheritance, which is the only form without social or legal restrictions; and this makes holdings continually decrease in size through fragmentation. Purchase is legal but not practical as the kinship group usually exerts great pressures on any member who tries to sell his share of land or a part of it. Some get around these constraints and conclude deals although the laws governing such transfers (especially the pre-emption right) require that the co-owners should be informed first.[9] The Pre-emption Ordinance of 1918 put the rights of co-owners first; and they have the right to retrieve the land to the *sagiya* group within six months from the date of purchase. It is the fact of corporate ownership in the *sagiya* that kept the agnatic descent group as a production unit until recently. The individual shares were known, though not identified as plots; this was a later development when it became possible for small plots to be brought under cultivation of a different kind – cash crops, especially dates and vegetables.

*miyri Land* This includes all land which was not possessed in 1905. Leasehold from the government has become the only form of possession since then. The acquisition of this type depends mainly on one's economic status and influence on the local administrators. To hold land in practice follows a successful application to install a pump, which demands the fulfilment of a number of requirements. First there is a certificate that one is able to 'utilize' the land. In the past this was decided by the Native Administration personnel; and to influence these was the target of agricultural investors. Now the licensing of pumps and lease of land are totally under the control of government local authorities on whom different means of influencing are used, such as gifts, feasts, etc. It is still necessary that a licensee 'should have sufficient capital to finance the proposed scheme',[10] a condition which the exercise of these means of influencing partly demonstrates.

Unlike the milk land, the *miyri* is not subjected to fragmentation as the only permitted form of registration is collective even if the plot is inherited by a large number after the death of the original leaseholder. Small plots leased to individuals cannot be divided and they are required to be cultivated as one unit. Little of the *miyri* land is heritable because most of it is now incorporated in larger units of production rather than being individually held. These production units are further removed from the ownership of the kinship group than was the case under the *sagiya*. *miyri* land is leased from the government and then sub-let to tenants in the schemes on behalf of the government whose major interest is that the land should be put to productive use. The moment the scheme fails to cultivate part or all of the land tied to it, then the land can be reappropriated to any eligible applicant, or in certain circumstances, as happened in the first two years of the present government, be tranformed into a co-operative scheme. The result of this policy was not encouraging to either the government or the tenants and since then it has been abandoned although until now the co-operatives are assisted in the distribution of consumer goods, but not in the production sphere. This has positively influenced a shift in the deployment of retailers' capital into agricultural and related services, a move which proves their success, to some extent; and consequently they could ask for assistance, which the government gives, especially since the performance of the co-operatives was not as convincing as that of the individual endeavours.

As I have stated before the *milk* land is limited in area and is constantly decreased by housing and river erosion, and it is not suitable for seasonal crop production since such activity requires relatively extensive areas that only the *miyri* land can allow for. Consequently most of the *milk* is now put under orchards or vegetable growing. A date tree does not need more than four square metres to grow and a considerable number of trees can be planted in a small plot; otherwise it can be put under vegetables to meet the family needs. The right to grow trees on *milk* is denied to non-owners of *milk* land except through an elaborate system of share-cropping arrangements which will be described in the next chapter. So we find that ownership of date trees, or any other permanent crops, like the ownership of the *milk* land itself, signifies that the owner is from the *ahali*, even though the owner might not own the land on which the trees are grown.

Although planting of permanent trees was legally forbidden on *miyri* land, some people could have obtained a special permit for trees whose lifetime is shorter than the period of lease, and which only those who are profit-motivated can venture on growing. So the importance of the *miyri* derives not from the same type of cultivation as that practised on *milk* land, but from its use for the production of cereals and cash crops such as *ful masri*, wheat, *dura*, tick peas, *hilba*, garlic, cumin and tomatoes. One important fact about *miyri* land is that there can be more than a threefold increase in the areas under use once the necessary capital for irrigation works and labour is found. Up to now it has been horizontally increased by the incorporation of new land.[11] However, its importance is growing rapidly, and from a single village, Mushu, that I have studied the *milk* land represents a proportionally insignificant part of the productive land. Until 1937 *milk* land was the only land under use. When a pump was installed that year some *miyri* land was incorporated in the scheme and the percentage of the *milk* land fell to 34.5% of the cultivated land. By 1973 it was only 13.8% of the village cultivated land (261 out of a total area of 1,875 *faddans*).[12] It is the ever-increasing utilization of this type of land that has contributed to the economic and social changes observed in that area in the period under study.

Also, there has been a change in the role and use of these two types of land. In the past, the *milk* land was the main productive asset but with the consequent expansion following the introduction of mechanical pumps vast areas in the *miyri* were brought under use. The *milk* land, then, is accorded a secondary productive role although its social role as identifying the *ahali* group and their status within a multi-ethnic situation is growing in importance. The *milk* land is still, however small it may be, eligible for mortgage loans from the Agricultural Bank; and this is itself an indicator of status, as it was until 1977 the only form of mortgage the bank would accept. Of course, some people have access to these loans with other types of security which the ordinary peasants cannot afford, for example the pump itself or date trees. Others, especially traders, can use loans from commercial banks which are advanced on different bases and with different conditions from those of the Agricultural Bank, and they do not necessarily demand a mortgage or at least, not in land.

From the above description we can see how the *miyri* is becoming the subject of increasing agricultural production in the region. It is, as I mentioned before, theoretically accessible to all, but practically, except in the case of agricultural co-operatives, access depends on the investor's, or investors', social and most importantly financial position. It is this fact which enabled the traders, both town merchants and village retailers, to start by installing *matarat*, that is small pumps or *sagiyas* on wells, in the past; and then later to install larger pumps individually or in partnerships.

**Section II Resources and organization of labour**

In this section only agricultural labour is described. The organization of farm work and the different labour resources are described in detail in the next chapter, as there is a close relationship between the type of work rendered and the system of reward which together constitute the core of the relations of production in the agricultural production.

Under the *sagiya* system of cultivation, the cultivator was assigned different roles depending on the property relationships prevailing. The general pattern which has been described with the kinship system approximates to the model type of combined property in land and labour, yet we have to bear in mind different situations specifically allowing for non-owners as well as owners to participate in agricultural activity.

The class of people who actually undertake cultivation are called *tarabla* (sing. *turbal*) who are not necessarily the owners of the land or capital, or of the means of irrigation (*sagiya* in the past and pumps in the present) although they can own this means. The *turbal's* main asset, which is the major contribution to production, is his labour although under the *sagiya* he might be able to contribute some capital assets, usually animals. There was under *sagiya* a senior *turbal*, known as *samad moiya*, who might own a share in the land and the waterwheel, and his role was to administer agricultural operations in the *sagiya*.[13]

In addition to the *tarabla*, there were two types of agricultural labourers, namely *jiygol* (agricultural and domestic labourer) and *aurwatti* (*sagiya* driver). They differed from *tarabla* in that they were rewarded in cash whereas *tarabla* are share-croppers. The *jiygol*, participated in cultivation sometimes as a *turbal* with a share of the crop, but his share was usually appropriated by his employer and he was given his stipulated wage instead. Another difference between these agricultural labourers and *tarabla* was that the former was not confined to agricultural work. They provided other domestic services, chopping firewood, carrying water, caring for the animals, etc. The roles of the three have always been changing together with the personnel who occupied these roles. The triad of *sagiya* owners, *tarabla* and agricultural labourers underwent great changes when large areas of land were put under cultivation and a larger number of *tarabla* were needed. This demand for *tarabla* worked favourably to elevate the lower ranks of the triad, that is, the *jiygols* and *aurwattis*, to become *tarabla*. The *tarabla* of the past, who were mainly from the *ahali* group, assumed the new status of *muzari'in* (tenant farmers) with different rights and duties from those of the *tarabla* under the *sagiya* system. The *aurwatti's* role almost disappeared with the *sagiya*, and the *jiygol* either changed into a *muzari'* (sing. of *muzari'in*) or disappeared from permanent agricultural work and participated in it only as casual labourers. The *sagiya* owners who were from the *ahali* group began to put their land under a different use from that under the *sagiya* systems. However, there was a tendency among the *ahali* to abandon farming and seek employment outside as migrant labour in Saudi Arabia and the Gulf states; this started in the beginning of the fifties and has been on the increase since. No statistical data for the whole area is available concerning outward migration but the figures from the study of Mushu village point to this tendency, and more and more the Arabs and the

Sudaniyya are taking the role of *muzari'in* in the village although in 1974 they still accounted for less than the total number of *muzari'in* in the village, as can be seen from the following table:

**Table III Composition of Mushu Muzari'in**

| Ethnic Group | No. of Muzari'in | % from the respective group | % of all Muzari'in |
|---|---|---|---|
| *ahali* | 53 | 19% | 54% |
| Arabs | 21 | 81% | 22% |
| Sudaniyya | 22 | 52% | 23% |
| Others | 1100% | 1% | |

Source: Mushu Village Census conducted by the writer in April-May-June 1974.

From this table we can see that although the *ahali* form the majority of the *muzari'in* (54%), yet we find the Arabs and the Sudaniyya are represented in this class far more than their ratios of the village population, that: 7.5% and 12% for the Arabs and Sudaniyya respectively, the *ahali* constituted 80% of the village population. Another point which supported the promotion of these agricultural workers who were originally from the Arabs, Sudaniyya or the impoverished *ahali* was the increasing number from the former groups to take up agriculture as tenants in the schemes (81% of the Arabs and 52% of the Sudaniyya in the village) whereas the tendency among the *ahali* was to drift away from agriculture (as 19% of them have done). This does not mean the change into tenants of all people who can, or potentially can, form the class of casual agricultural labourers in the area. Still there are people who perform casual wage labour in agriculture and other services in the villages and these sometimes draw from the *muzari'in* class itself especially during periods of less agricultural work. Following the abortive land reform of the late sixties,[14] we have a situation where agricultural labourers (not only casual workers but in some schemes tenants themselves) are getting ever scarcer.

Under the *sagiya* and the earlier stages of the pump schemes agricultural wage-labourers were sufficient to meet the demands of the then agricultural production. The present casual labour is provided mostly by the tenants themselves, although there are still some Sudaniyya who move about in the region and perform one form or another of casual wage-labour, and sometimes engage in agricultural wage-labour either for those tenants who prefer hired labour to the communal labour of the co-tenants, or in big individual agricultural schemes where dates and citrus fruits are cultivated and necessitate the employment of permanent and casual hired labour. These hired labourers do not specialize in any specific agricultural or other work. One may for example work threshing *dura* in November and December, and engage in whitewashing houses in April and May, but not participate in wheat harvesting which takes place then. Also the development of large scale production created more demand for seasonal labour. This demand started increasing when flood irrigation began in 1909 in the

Northern Province in general and Dongola District in particular. The demand declined a little shortly before the Second World War. In that period radical changes were effected in the methods of irrigation, which demanded more workers than the village could provide.

The changes in the pattern of casual labour traditionally provided by the nomadic Arabs on a seasonal basis started in that period. These nomads began to settle gradually on the fringes of the villages and provide the necessary agricultural labour as *jiygols* or *tarabla*. This started with those nomads who before settling had long-standing relationships with the villagers. In this stage, which coincided with the first phase of the schemes (See next chapter, section III), a relationship of a patron-client type emerged and it continued until the beginning of the seventies. These relationships were maintained so as to provide for the patron a secure source of wage-labour when he needed it and at the same time guaranteeing a permanent source of cash for the client.

At present such personal ties, symbolized by the term *jiygol*, do not exist for a number of reasons, chief among which are the way agricultural work is organized and the legal prohibition on the allocation of tenancies of the schemes to those who do not actually cultivate. As I have shown, this has influenced the position of the former *jiygols* and *aurwattis*, and to some extent that of the *tarabla* who are now independent *muzari'in* in the schemes. This economic improvement has not gone without significant consequences on the social and political status of the *jiygols* and *aurwattis* who derived mainly from the nomadic settlers, the Sudaniyya and the poor *ahali*. The dependency relationships which existed between the rich *ahali* as the landed class and providers of irrigation on one side and the Arabs, Sudaniyya and landless *ahali* on the other, have given way to new forms of relationships and also to new forms of farm work organization.

*Organization of Farm Work*

The farmer's work pattern is largely determined by the type of crop grown, its stage of growth, and the season of the year. These also determine when a *muzari'* needs labour and how much.

There are two major agricultural seasons. The *shitta* (winter) begins in October-November and extends over March and April. The main crops here are wheat and *ful masri* (horse beans) with some vegetables, chief among them onions and tomatoes. The *sayf* extends from May-June to October-November. The main crop here is *dura* and other summer vegetables and beans. There are two other seasons which are not important to the farmer's work, *dammiyra*, which is the flooding season of the Nile in July, August and September; and *rabiy'* (spring) which includes parts of March and April.

Contrary to the *sagiya* system which had many *tarabla* in a plot of ten *faddans*, we find that the pattern in the schemes now usually five-*faddan* plots cultivated by a couple of tenants. The selection of the co-farmer is left to the senior *muzari'*.[15] The plot is cultivated with wheat and *ful masri* in winter, followed by *dura* in summer. After the harvesting of the *dura* it is left fallow for a whole year and then cultivated with wheat. The land is cultivated in a double rotation – by having two successive crops on one piece and then leaving it fallow for a whole year while work is shifted to another plot within the same scheme. So tenants establish no identification with a specific plot as they shift from one plot to another according to the plans of the scheme's administration.[16] The work on these tenancies is now discussed under co-tenants work, family work, and *faza'a* or communal work.

a. *Co-tenants' work* The use of cattle in many of the agricultural operations has reduced the amount of human labour expended by the tenants. In the past sowing and clearing of the land demanded much hoeing, which necessitated the collaboration of many hands. Now the use of an iron plough instead of the hoe, and the use of the *noraj*, a threshing machine, have caused a more efficient combination of human and animal energy in the performance of much of the agricultural work. Clearing, levelling, sowing, ploughing and threshing were formerly done by the muzari'cin. Now a plough or threshing machine can be hired if it is not owned by the tenants. Further, deep tractor ploughing is carried out by the schemes on the fallow land every year; this facilitates most of the agricultural operations as well as contributing to the fertility of the soil. So the tenant's work is to administer the use of these implements, owned or hired, and the irrigation of the plot. He provides the human labour necessary for all operations and in return he is entitled to half of the product after deducting the shared costs of ploughing, seeds, threshing, etc. The tenant can use hired labour not to replace him in work but to assist at peak seasons if communal labour is impractical.

b. *Family work* The family role in agricultural production has been steadily declining. Under *sagiya* cultivation, family members used to provide more work than they do today. The *aurwatti*, for example, was sometimes a junior member of the extended family who was too young or too weak to participate in other tasks. The wife's work is becoming increasingly confined to domestic work although she may still provide fodder for the milk sheep and goats of the household, or may rear her animals in the fallow lands helped by her younger children if they are not busy at school.

Now the major tasks of the wife on the field are weeding and cutting off the ears of *dura* (*kiddaig*) after the stalks are cut down by the men. For the wheat crop she helps with the *dolaig* (collection of fallen ears of grain); and sometimes hulling. No more work is assigned to her in the field except the clearing of the *tagga* (threshing place) and the bringing of her husband's food when he is occupied in irrigation or any other job.

Children's work is more limited. They usually help with their mothers' tasks in the field. They help in the rearing of animals and sometimes help the father in bird scaring.

c. *faza'a or Work Party*[17] The *faza'a* which is known as *nafir* in central and western parts of the Sudan is limited to a few agricultural tasks – those which demand many hands in a short time like the cutting of wheat and *dura*. Developments in agricultural techniques, and the use of hired labour, are gradually replacing *faza'a*.

The use of *faza'a* is conditioned by different factors. For example, *dura* threshing which is done by beating the heads of grain with sticks was formerly done by *faza'a*, but now is mostly done by hired labour. But wheat cutting is still accomplished by *faza'a* as it demands speed, lest the ears should fall. Moreover, returns from *dura* are less than those from the wheat. So when the cost of food (which includes the slaughtering of a he-goat) and drinks (*mariysa* – local date beer) for the party is less than the payment for what hired labour would be, a *faza'a* would likely be used. Wheat cutting needs more workers at once as most of the wheat ripens at the same time. If left for long, many of the grains will fall as the stalks get drier; they also become a prey to birds which are difficult to scare over a large area. Alternative precautions may be used to lessen the damage to the wheat crop. Some tenant farmers sow their wheat at intervals of five to ten days which will make it ripen at intervals, and hence lessen the bird menace as scaring could be concentrated in one part of the field. This also eases cutting as they can spread it over a longer time and hence do not need the assistance of *faza'a* or hired labour.

**Section III Capital Resources and Agricultural Investment**

Capital is used here to refer to the financial resources for investment in agriculture. It has traditionally been important for two different but closely related and complementary activities, namely the provision of irrigational equipment and land reclamation on the one hand, and to furnish the necessary agricultural credit on the other. While the first type comes from different sources from within the area and outside, capital for agricultural credit, mainly comes from internal resources of the villages or from big merchants of the rural towns, depending on the amount required and the nature of the operations to be financed.[18]

a. *Government as a Source of Capital* Until the mid-thirties all major irrigational works in the then Dongola Province (the present Northern Province and parts of the present Nile Province)[19] were provided by the colonial governments.[20] After the Re-Occupation the government was faced with the problem of feeding the increasing numbers of settling Danagla who had been either involved in the Mahdiyya wars or fled from its demands. The Danagla were encouraged to rebuild their *sagiyas* and those who did were exempted from crop taxes for a year.[21] As a further measure all land under individual titles was fully taxed if it was not cultivated, which encouraged owners to cultivate it.[22] At the same time the colonial administration was pre-occupied with the problem of increasing production by introducing more efficient means of irrigation to replace the *sagiyas*, a problem which was solved in other parts of the then one province by installing pump schemes. In Dongola, the Suleim basin was opened in 1909 with an area of 24,000 *faddans*, of which 37,270[23] are under cultivation by smallholder tenant farmers. When this scheme started, the Danagla were reluctant to cultivate the land of the basin which they considered far away from their residential settlements along the banks of the river. A number of Egyptian fellahin as well as some Shaiqiya, Mahas, and nomads, who were encouraged to settle and carry on agriculture as well as continuing to keep some of their animals,[24] were all imported into the scheme.

The second major government investment was the Burgeig pump scheme established in 1944 in the northern part of the Suleim basin. A large number of the tenants in this scheme also were brought in from outside Dongola area. This, as well as the reluctance of the riverain settlers to move in, points to the fact that the area was short of agricultural labour. This shortage was partly due to the departure of slaves, as argued by al-Shahi, but more importantly it was because of the big rate of expansion of agriculture along the river banks which absorbed the existing labour resources.[25]

Apart from a small pilot dairy farm in a disputed island which was taken over by the government in 1971, the government has not been engaged in any massive form of agricultural investment in the region since the establishment of the Burgeig scheme in 1944. However, the intention of the present government is to invest more in the province, which is showing serious financial difficulties (local resources accounted only for 10% of the province's budget in 1976/7) as well as severe deficiencies in food crops. The tendency to cultivate cash crops in the Suleim basin and most of the schemes of the area necessitated the importation of food cereals from Central Sudan. The government is planning a number of agricultural schemes to provide for local needs and produce a surplus, as well as to create employment and so lessen the high rate of emigration. The following are the schemes which have been studied and await financing in Dongola District:[26]

| | |
|---|---|
| al-Khawiy scheme | 200,000 faddans |
| Gharb el-Golid | 29,000 faddans |
| Akkad scheme | 27,000 faddans |
| Kooka scheme | 5,000 faddans |
| Burgeig scheme extension | 5,000 faddans |
| TOTAL | 266,000 faddans |

Although the planned schemes will more than double the existing area under cultivation, we find that only about one fifth of the already protected land is under use.[27] However Danagla agriculture needs more financial help than the governmental and quasi-governmental institutions like the Agricultural Bank had already provided. Government action, when involved, was directed to the provision of irrigation or allocation of land to different eligible applicants. In the sphere of actual production neither the government in its sponsored schemes nor the private schemes, with the exception of a few co-operatives with reserve funds, provide any loans for the undertaking of agricultural operations or short loans to assist the tenant producers with their consumption needs in the pre-harvest period. This sphere of agricultural credit is totally dominated by the traders in the villages and towns of the region, who have been able to accumulate large amounts of money from the interests on these advances, locally known as *shayl* and *rammiya*. This form of accumulation, especially for beginner traders in the past, enabled them to reinvest in more trade, in agricultural production by installing *sagiyas* and pumps, or in providing more *shayl* to the tenants and peasant farmers alike.[28]

Tenant farmers have two different sets of relations with capital whereas peasant farmers, except for some in the Suleim, have only one, that of credit. The first relation for the tenant is that with the capital used for investment in land acquisition and the provision of irrigation. The second, which is shared with the peasant farmer, and some small pump owners who are not cultivators, is where the tenant needs it to furnish agricultural credit. The first is directly related to the relations of production and the basis of share-cropping, while the second is independent of the first and relates mostly to the sphere of circulation of agricultural and other market goods. It is in this relationship that all agricultural producers, irrespective of the form of the production relations or the ownership of the means of production, may in one way or another be related to credit-advancing bodies, among which the chief (and until 1962 the sole) is the traders, through the *shayl* system.

This analytical division of capital will enable us to discern the type of relations that prevail in the production process and those which embrace other social elements which are not directly related to that process, and how these two sets of relations influence the social structure of the Danagla, i.e. the relationships between the different ethnic and tribal groups that constitute Danagla society. The next chapter will deal with the problem of the relations of production resulting from the working of the productive capital, and in the last chapter of this book I will consider merchant capital and its consequences both to the owners and to those who are provided with it.

b. *Other Sources of Capital* As I have stated in the introduction the capital necessary for land reclamation and investment in irrigation equipment has largely been furnished by private entrepreneurs, peasant savings and emigrants' remittances from abroad, which, especially in the mid-thirties, provided the major part of the financial requirements of the then developing Agricultural Co-operative Companies of the Northern Province.[29]

These co-operative companies added to the already existing private and governmental schemes in the then Northern Province but in Dongola area all the schemes before the Burgeig (1944) were private pumps. The capital necessary to install these earlier private schemes, plus many which were established later, had been furnished from trade or migrant labour outside the area, especially in Egypt. Peasant savings were negligible and were not sufficient, under *sagiya* cultivation, to provide the capital necessary for a pump. However, a few managed, helped by their migrant relatives, to reinvest in agriculture by installing more *sagiyas* or replacing them with pumps. For the local farmer it was not easy to make much surplus from *sagiya* agriculture as it was not efficient or economical when used for large areas of land. Since it depended on animal power, most of the cultivation consisted of fodder and hence there could only be a narrow margin of profit or savings. Nevertheless, ownership of date trees combined with remittances from relatives allowed some of the resident peasants to hold shares in the developing co-operatives, or to afford the use of hired labour.[30] This is most characteristic of the family partnerships which install small pumps with the intention of irrigating their *milk* land and the date and citrus trees grown on it. These pumps as I have pointed out in Chapter 3 are joint ventures to reproduce the *sagiya* and the kinship unit owning it rather than effectively contributing to the expansion of agricultural production.

Apart from such savings and remittances very few individuals who were not traders were engaged in agricultural investment. Two people of Egyptian origin were given relatively large areas of land in 1916 (about 1,622 faddans between them).[31] One of them was the local leader of a religious sect, the Idriysiya, and the other was an army medical assistant. Later in the late thirties, the head of the Native Administration in Dongola was given a scheme in the area making, until 1940, the only three pump schemes which were owned neither by the co-operative companies nor by traders. At present only the last of these three is in the hands of its original owner. The religious leader's scheme changed hands; it is now owned individually by a merchant from the Falaliyh group and is one of the biggest schemes in Dongola. The other changed into a co-operative in the mid-sixties after the death of its original owner. All other private schemes that followed were partnerships between relatives, or agricultural companies run on a commercial basis, or co-operative societies (or co-operative companies before the 1948 Co-operation Ordinance).

c. *Co-operation and Provision of Capital* Co-operation in this area derives its importance mainly from two activities in agriculture. It is directly concerned with the process of production by the provision of pumping equipment, and agricultural equipment such as tractors; the other role is indirect, that is the promotion and development of the villages in which they are situated.[32]

For the first function the emphasis is on the purchase of irrigation equipment and reclamation of land. The second objective relates to the distribution of the products of the co-operatives especially in the case of the earlier co-operative companies when these were not regarded as the concern of the shareholders only but that of the whole village. Now the part played by the co-operatives with respect to the second role has been minimized as more rules, and interference by the co-operation department, make it difficult for indigenous practices which are now illegal under co-operative regulations.

The earlier co-operatives were not much concerned with post-production operations such as storage and marketing, nor were they concerned with the provision of agricultural credit. These two activities were monopolized by traders and formed the basis of their capital accumulation and its investment and reinvestment in agriculture and trade.

At the time of fieldwork for this study (1976/77) there was a total of 96 co-operative societies registered in the regional Co-operation Office. The development of these co-operatives started with the agricultural co-operative companies of the mid-thirties and these were later, especially after 1970, joined by a number of consumer goods co-operatives and multi-purpose societies which are mainly concentrated in the towns of Dongola, Argo and Kerma (See Table IV).

When the agricultural co-operatives started in the area, there had been already a number of private individual and company schemes. So the co-operative companies:

> . . . joined a long list of pump schemes run by the government, partnerships, private companies and individuals, but they were the first whose structure was related to the financial means of the small holder while at the same time guaranteeing them a measure of control.[33]

**Table IV Co-operative Societies in Dongola District 1976/7**

| Council[1] | Agricultural Co-operatives | Flour Mills** | Tractors** Co-operatives | Multipurpose Co-operatives | Consumer Co-operatives | Total |
|---|---|---|---|---|---|---|
| | No. | No. | No. | No. | No. | |
| El-Golid | 20 | 1 | 1— | 1 | — | 22 |
| Dongola | 12 | 1 | — | 6 | 2 | 21 |
| Argo | 30 | 7 | 2 | 13 | 1 | 53 |
| Total | 62 | 9 | 2 | 20 | 3 | 96 |
| | (64.58%) | (9.37%) | (2.08%) | (20.83%) | (3.1%) | 96 |

* *Source: 1975/76 Annual Report*, Assistant Commissioner for Co-operation, Dongola.

** Flour mills and tractors are usually owned by existing agricultural co-operatives. So we can say that Agricultural Co-operatives represent about 76% of the co-operatives in the region.

1 The Northern part of the district (Argo People's Rural Council) has the majority of co-operatives. The people here were the first to migrate and to start co-operatives.

However, the control over co-operatives is a controversial issue as the peasants (referred to as smallholders) could not raise the capital which mostly came from migrants and local shopkeepers nor were they experienced enough to handle the administration when co-operatives were established. So control of the co-operatives was in the hands of the existing local leaders who dominated them as an extension to their authority within the villages until changes started to emerge in the early 1970s. These changes influenced not only the control over the co-operatives but also the relations of production in both co-operative and non-co-operative agricultural schemes. These developments which shaped the present co-operatives' performance came later, but here reference is made to earlier regulations issued to improve the administration of the co-operatives and the supervision of their performance. In 1948, the Co-operative Societies Ordinance was issued and many of the previous practices rendered illegal.[34] Before this ordinance the co-operatives, in legal situations, were considered as commercial companies and governed by the 1925 Companies Ordinance. Internally none of the characteristics of company administration were practised and as a matter of fact not even in the registered commercial agricultural companies in the area. The administration followed the initial practice, and consensus of the villagers seemed to constitute the major criterion for the selection of governing boards of the societies. In that capacity the societies were additional channels for the reinforcement of political positions within the villages' political, social and economic organization. Presumably the continuation of some of the co-operative companies as commercial companies after the 1948 Ordinance was because of the threat the new rules posed to the authority of the traditional leaders.[35] Most of the co-operative companies remained as companies whereas most of the co-operatives of today were established in the period following the 1948 Co-operatives Ordinance. Of six co-operative schemes studied with other types of schemes one was established in 1945 and the five others were established in the period 1951–9.[36]

*Agricultural Co-operatives: Performance and Control Work for Uniformity* Successive national governments tried to encourage co-operative societies so as to increase agricultural production in the Northern Province in the hope that this would lessen outward migration and contribute to the welfare of the rural population. In 1960 a branch of the Agricultural Bank of the Sudan opened in Dongola to help cultivators in the region and especially those in co-operative schemes. The positive policies of the bank in advancing loans made the co-operatives flourish after a long period of failures due to lack of funds for further developments and replacement of machinery. By the mid-sixties the co-operative schemes were reported to be standing on their feet and making progress:

> . . . because of the strict supervision of the co-operation office over co-operative schemes, especially in financial affairs; and the facilities the office obtained for them from the Agricultural Bank, it could be said that the co-operative schemes are the most successful in the region. They have good administration and satisfactory production. Next to them are the individual private schemes, while the commercial companies are in the third place.[37] (My translation).

However this situation was reversed during the following ten years to the extent that some *milk* land-owners withdrew their land from the co-operatives because of their inability to provide regular irrigation either on account of the *kodaig*,[38] or mechanical failures;

> . . . with respect to area, the co-operative schemes come first and are followed in the second place by individual private schemes and by the companies in the third place. Moreover, the co-operatives hold twice as much land as that held by the other two types of schemes. Nevertheless, they are characterized by bad administration and insufficient irrigation. This has made people withdraw their lands from the co-operatives and install private pumps on them.[39] (My translation).

It is characteristic of all annual reports of the co-operation office in the last five years to point to the bad administration and other technical and natural obstacles to the functioning of co-operatives. However, the mechanical and natural difficulties are faced by other schemes also, but these have got the means to solve the problems by access to sufficient financial resources, either individually or institutionally (from banks) to which the co-operatives have limited access.

The problems of the co-operatives which are very complicated cannot be discussed in detail here but we can point to some indicators of weaknesses in them, administratively and financially. In the six co-operatives studied they actually cultivated around 1,005 *faddans* in 1976/77 out of a total of 2,282, that is 44%, whereas in the individual schemes 1108.5 *faddans* were cultivated out of 1350.45 *faddans*, 82%, in the same year. (See Table V).

**Table V Summary of Characteristics of Co-operatives in the sample studied**

| Name of Co-operative and date of registration | Capital* | Area of* Land in faddans | Area cultivated in faddans | % | No. of tenancies | No. of tenants | No. of* Shareholders | Attendance at* last meeting | % |
|---|---|---|---|---|---|---|---|---|---|
| Shaykh Shariyf South (1952) | s£ 3,800 | 456 fad. | 140 fad. | 30.7 | 21 | 21 | 335 | 27 | 8 |
| El-Tayiti (1957) | s£ 4,953 | 450 fad. | 150 fad. | 31 | 11 | 11 | 300 | 50 | 16.6 |
| Sugdan (1951) | s£15,439 | 536 fad. (All milk) | 380 fad. | 70 | 62 | 98 | 520 | 120 | 23 |
| Koyya el-Aradayba (1956) | s£ 880 | 125 fad. | — | — | — | — | 75 | 20 | 26.6 |
| Sowri (1945) | s£ 2,040 | 515 fad. | 170 fad. | 33 | 38 | 30 | 242 | 33 | 13-6 |
| Salagi (1959) | s£ 914 | 200 fad. | 165 fad. | 82 | 15 | 17 | 70 | 22 | 31.4 |
| TOTAL | 28,026 | 2,282 | 1,005 | 44 | 147 | 177 | 1,542 | 272 | 17.6 |

* *Information compiled from the Societies respective files: Assistant Commission for Cooperation, Dongola 1977.*

| | | | |
|---|---|---|---|
| Capital investment per faddan | s£12.28 | Capital invest per cultivated faddan | s£27.89 |
| Total land over shareholders | 1.47 faddan/shareholder | Cultivated land by shareholder | 0.55 faddans |
| Total land over cultivator | 12.89 faddan/tenant | Cultivated land/tenant | 5.67 faddans |
| Possible size of tenancy | 15.52 faddans | Size of tenancy | 6.83 faddans |

The decline of co-operatives and their failure to achieve their objectives, however, has been explained differently by specialists especially those of the regional co-operation office. They usually attribute the failures to the lack of agricultural workers, canal clearing, and bad administration but never question the adequacy of the co-operative rules and supervision which, together with the lack of financial resources, contributed to the failures. Farah Hassan Adam pointed to these failures:

1. the smallness of land and its unsuitability for collective production,
2. the co-operative shareholders were not the actual cultivators and agricultural labourers. Moreover shareholding was a function of land ownership and other financial resources which made co-operatives to be established by the small village shopkeepers, government officials, and others who had other resources outside the region,
3. most of the co-operatives were established to own and run the irrigation equipment, leaving the co-operating members to live the way they like,

4. the absence of co-operative education, and finally,
5. the failure of most of the co-operatives' initiative which precipitated a negative attitude.[40] (My translation)

Of the above reasons I think the second and the third are very important in influencing the performance of co-operatives, and because of their subtle nature they are hardly explainable by the regional co-operation officials. However, I am not going to discuss the problems of co-operatives at length here, but I must point to the fact that in the early seventies intensive politicization of co-operatives, in addition to other reforms and preferences, contributed directly to the decline of co-operatives in the last five or six years. It was the imposition of political ideals on the co-operatives (like regarding them as colleges for local and national elections) that deprived them of their former economic and social objectives set by the people who initiated them prior to governmental intervention. Alternatively they have been changed into platforms of political conflicts which lessen their efficiency. The co-operative used to be the supplier of food crops to the whole village irrespective of membership of tenancy holders. The identification of every village with a particular co-operative society extends the corporateness of the village into that of the co-operative, and consequently the co-operative was put to the benefit of all villagers villagers irrespective of membership. The harvest time is not only harvest time for the tenants and shareholders but also for all the non-member villagers.[41] Only after the village requirements had been met was the surplus taken to the market.[42] Now the priority is to get the higher cash returns from the share of the co-operative society, which is justifiable under present conditions; but this, I think, has been replacing the support the co-operative would need for raising funds and meeting some urgent financial needs. The traditional leaders of the co-operatives (who are mainly traders and people who command more economic and social resources than the ordinary tenant would possess) lost interest in them as they became too far removed from their control and hence they see no justification for their financial and personal support, which they can invest more profitably elsewhere. At the same time the emerging new leaders are lacking in both the experience and the resources to help the co-operative to function in the absence of substantial government support. Hence the continous reference to bad administration and insufficient irrigation while other schemes which have not been affected are counted now as the most successful. Here I am not advocating the continued control by traders of the administration of co-operatives nor their control over the marketing of co-operative products. But under present circumstances, it seems more satisfactory to attempt to undertake reform with substantial financial help so that the exploitative practices of the traders and money lenders are eliminated, than to compel co-operative production to go into continuous decline leading to the liquidation of the existing co-operative societies. However, traders are still in a position to appropriate the co-operative products in the marketing sphere where no serious attempt has been made by the co-operation office to change it.[43] The traders retained their strong control over the co-operatives and other institutions in the area, by being the only marketing channel of agricultural products, providers of credit and, to some extent, competitors with the co-operatives through their own private pumps and partnerships. Yet a substantial number of traders are still members of the governing boards of co-operatives and the main suppliers of agricultural credit and *shayl* to the tenants of both co-operatives and other schemes. Although the Agricultural Bank is supposed to provide these loans for the co-operative societies and tenants instead of traders, the demand for a fixed asset as mortgage worked against this as the figures in Table VI show:

## Table VI
## Loans advanced by Agricultural Bank for Co-operatives and Individuals (1965/1970)

| Year | 1965/6 | | 1966/67 | | 1967/8 | | 1968/9 | | 1969/70 | | Total | | Average per loan £s |
|---|---|---|---|---|---|---|---|---|---|---|---|---|---|
| | Qty | Value in £s | Qty | Value in £s | Qty | Value in £s | Qty | Value in £s | Qty | Value in £s | Qty | Value in £s | |
| Co-operatives | 15 | 21203 | 6 | 4939 | — | — | — | — | 3 | 7358 | 24 | 33500 | 1395.8 |
| Individuals | 19 | 18542 | 24 | 23178 | 17 | 27754 | 17 | 23097 | 114 | 17153 | 191 | 1097 | 574 |

**Source:** *Annual Reports*, Agricultural Bank of Sudan, Dongola.

It can be seen that loans to individuals are greater in number than those of the co-operatives and are steadily on the increase whereas loans to co-operatives are few and decreasing. On the other hand the co-operative loans, when advanced, are larger than individual loans (£s1395 on average as against £s574 for individual loans). This is because individual schemes are smaller and hence smaller loans are required for the financing of agricultural operations, fuel and spare parts. The advantage of individuals as regards the bank's loans derives from the fact that they can provide mortgage in the form of date trees and other property whereas the co-operatives get loans only when guaranteed by the government, i.e. the co-operation authorities — a guarantee which is seldom obtained. This is a situation which explains the dependence of some co-operatives (probably the most successful of them) on the traders to run them despite the grievances of the tenants and those of the local co-operation authorities. The domination of co-operatives by traders worried the officials and hence their efforts to invoke higher levels of authorities against the traders as the following extracts from their letters reveal:

> The holding of key positions by traders in co-operative societies as chairmen, secretaries and treasurers constitutes a major threat to the future of co-operative societies. This is due to their commercial expertise which puts them in a position to control their villages. Furthermore, by being responsible for the co-operatives, they are able to appropriate the products of the societies both from the societies and the tenants.[44] (My translation).

A year later the same manager wrote about the poor performance and the marketing problems of the co-operatives;

> The members of the boards of some co-operative societies are traders and these co-operatives have no dealings with the Union (the Khandaq Co-operative Union) but instead these traders purchase the products themselves for personal gain.[45] (My translation).

I have dealt with these co-operative problems as they are very important for the analysis of both capital for agricultural investment, and the provision of credit for the tenant cultivators, showing the limitations of co-operatives, at least at present, to fulfil either of the two functions. Traders and other private individuals as local financiers are more important than either the government agencies like the agricultural and co-operation regional offices, or the semi-governmental institutions like the Agricultural Bank. Their role in financing both investments and credits will be described in Chapter Six.

## Notes

1 Chapters 5 and 6.
2 *milk subtypes:* a) old islands; b) *jarf;* c) *saluka* and d) *sagiya* land which may incorporate some *miyri* land. *miyri subtypes:* a) newly appearing islands; b) some of the *sagiya* land acquired by *hag al gusad* (right of frontage) and c) *karoo* which is totally *miyri*. See glossary for the meanings of the different types. (See also Fig. II, p.68.)
3 P. M. Holt, *Modern History of the Sudan*, London 1963, p.118
4 M. I. Abu Salim, *al-Ard fi al-Mahdiyya*, Sudan Research Unit, University of Khartoum, 1971, p.21.
5 No statistical information is available for the region, but in one village that I studied in 1974/5, 33% of the *ahali* group did not have any holdings in *milk*, yet many had holding in the *miyri* land.
6 *Register of Agada Land*, Dongola Land Registration Office, 1972.
7 J. W. Hewison, 'Northern Province Agriculture' in *Agriculture in the Sudan*, edited by J. D. Tothill, Oxford, 1952, p.748; where he showed the difficulties in all government schemes in the then Northern Province. Also see cases documented by H. Dafalla further to the north where there were very tiny holdings such as 0.0004 (1.7 sq.m.) of a faddan in 1969. Hassan Dafalla, 'Land Economy of Old Halfa', in *Sudan Notes and Records*, Vol. 50, 1969, p.64.
8 See the definition of *sagiya* in Chapter 1.
9 To register land under a different name from that of the original owner or heirs, certain rules should be observed: i) the deal should be a purchase and not a gift; ii) land should be free from obstacles to registration, local taxes, for example, iii) a suitable price has been agreed on; iv) the buyer should be Sudanese; v) the village *shaykh* should judge the seller to be mentally sound, etc. *A Memorandum on the Registration of Land*, 1964, Dongola Land Registration Office.
10 Land Registration Ordinance No. 29, 'The Nile Pump Control (General) Regulations, A Memorandum to District Commissioners', *Sudan Gazette*, 1964, p.28.
11 It is difficult to have reliable statistics on the developments in this type of land. It has been estimated that over a quarter of a million *faddans* can be brought under cultivation in the next ten years. *Annual Report 1976/77*, Assistant Commissioner for Agricultural Affairs, Dongola.
12 *Files of Mushu Commercial Scheme and Kamneya Co-operative Scheme;* Private Pumps Office, Dongola.
13 A *samad moiya* is different from samad *sagiya* who is not necessarily a cultivator and represents the *sagiya* owners both to the authorities for the collection of taxes, and to the *tarabla*.
14 One of the provisions was that tenancies should only be allocated to people who actually undertake cultivation; also no single tenant should hold more than one plot.
15 Under present arrangements this senior tenant is not entitled to any material benefits, unlike the *samad moiya* in the *sagiya* system. (See next chapter, Section III).
16 This pattern of rotation does not exist in the Suleim basin or the Burgeig government scheme. There the tenancies are fixed and permanent and the implementation of a rotational system is achieved within individual tenancies.
17 Faz'a is an institution whereby a working group is formed from the tenants of the scheme to finish agricultural tasks which need much co-operation. It can extend also to non-agricultural work like house maintenance (roofing in particular) but still follows the tenants' co-operation in the scheme (non-tenants have these works done by hired labour). Because of the differences in the economic organization in this part of the country, this form of co-operation is slightly different from the *nafir*, described by Holy and

Ahmed for Western and Central Sudan, whose members are recruited mainly on a cognatic kinship or neighbourly basis. For the *nafir* see L. Holy, *Neighbours and Kinsmen; A study of the Berti People of Darfur*, London, 1974, pp.80/84; and Abdul Ghaffar M. Ahmed, *Economic Anthropology and Problems of Development in the Sudan* (in Arabic) Khartoum University Press, 1975, p.81.

18 There is a branch of the Agricultural Bank of the Sudan in Dongola whose credit is mainly given against security of one kind or another which only those who are already wealthy could provide.

19 See Map

20 A number of pump schemes were installed during and after the first World War in Ghaba, Gureir, Kulud, and Nuri, none of which was in the area under consideration. Apart from the flood irrigation in the Suleim and Letti basins in the early days the government did not make any agricultural investment until 1944 when the Burgeig scheme was established.

21 *Sudan Gazette*, No. 46, April 1903.

22 Al-Shahi, *op.cit.*, p.132.

23 Abdul Mutalib, *op.cit.*, Table 5.

24 To provide pasture for their animals a whole section of the basin (Qism I) was left as grazing land. It is no longer flooded as a result of the creeping sand, but there are some *matarat* in it.

25 Al-Shahi argued, following the early administrative reports of 1906–7–8, that the departure of slaves had caused the problem of lack of agricultural labourers (al-Shahi, p.132). But we must accept the fact that the vacuum was quickly filled by the Danagla taking agricultural work themselves. As I have stated elsewhere, slaves were mainly occupied in cultivation but only in hazardous works, domestic or agricultural. Moreover, very few *ahali* had slaves. The marked shortage of labour then did not occur following the formal declaration of the abolition of slavery at the beginning of colonial rule, but in the period from the mid-twenties to the early forties when extensive agricultural production by the government, and the private and co-operative schemes, were inaugurated. This is the period when the nomadic tribes and the Egyptian fellahin were accommodated in the Danagla economy.

26 *Annual Report 1976/7*, Assistant Commissioner for Agriculture Affairs, Dongola.

27 It is reported that the total area registered by the pump schemes along the river banks is 131,743 faddans. No exact figures of areas cultivated for all the schemes are available but in the co-operative schemes out of 31,557 faddans registered only 11,661 faddans (37%) were under use in 1969/70; see *Annual Report 1969/70*, Agricultural Bank of the Sudan, Dongola. In the Suleim basin the situation is different where 37,270 faddans (72%) were cultivated out of 51,630 faddans in the same year. See Abdul Mutalib, *op.cit.*

28 I use tenant farmer and peasant farmer to differentiate between two patterns of production. The first is where the cultivator is a tenant in a scheme. In the second, especially in Suleim after 1970, the farmer apparently owns his means of irrigation and land.

29 There are no statistics showing the number of migrants but all reference to migration has usually been based on impressions. However, the study of Mushu village in 1974 showed that 404 (20%) out of the total population of 2,014 are living outside the village. For the whole area the following figures may show the impact of migrationon the sex ratio:

| | | |
|---|---|---|
| Male population | 71,747 | (44.8%) |
| Female population | 88,282 | (55.2%) |

30 J. W. Hewison, Northern Province Agriculture; in J. D. Tothill (ed.) *Agriculture in the Sudan*, 1948, p.756.

31 H. M. A. Sharfi, *A Directory to Merowe-Dongola District (in Arabic)*, Khartoum, 1957, p.47.

32 The last of these roles had not been incorporated in earlier objectives for co-operation in 1948. However it was embodied in the first indigenous organization of co-operatives.

33 See Manfred Bardeleben, *The Co-operative System in the Sudan*, Munchen, 1973, p.31.

34 The main rules of the Ordinance were that the society should submit its name for registration, objectives, purpose of fund raising, qualifications for admission, mode of election, number of members, receipts of money due or payable to society, and so on. But it was difficult to give up the type of co-operation practised in the area (mainly borrowed from Egypt and interwoven into local usage), for the sake of the rules drafted for the colonies by the Colonial Office (See Bardeleben, *op.cit.*, p.32), and codified in the 1948 Ordinance.

35 An example was the Mushu Co-operative Company which continued to hold this name until 1952. When approached to follow the regulations and register as a co-operative society, the immediate reaction was to declare the scheme a commercial company and change its name to 'Mushu Commercial and Development Company.'

36 Special pump schemes sample survey conducted by the writer in 1977 for the Economic and Social Research Council, Khartoum. (unpublished).

37 *Annual Report 1964/1965*, Private Pumps Office, Dongola.

38 Sands which block the canal bringing water to the site of the sucking pipes. Sometimes a large island may appear which is impossible to remove by the work of the tenants.

39 *Annual Report 1975/76*, Assistant Commissioner for Agricultural Affairs, Northern Province, Dongola.

40 Farah H. Adam et al, *On the Modernization of Agricultural Production in the Northern Region (The Northern and Nile Provinces)*. The Erkowit 9th Annual Conference, Karima, Institute of Extra-Mural Studies, University of Khartoum, 1976, p.11 (in Arabic).

41 There was a system by which the share of the co-operative was distributed to the village households who were not cultivators (*akkala* literally meaning 'eaters') at below market price. Now regulations do not allow this and higher prices are expected either by storage for a while, or directly selling in the market for the highest possible price.

42 This did not include the surpluses of the tenant cultivators which are mostly appropriated by traders through the *shayl* relationship.

43 In 1962 the Khandaq Co-operative Union was established and since then has concentrated its activities in fuel and spare parts supplies and not post-production operations. It started as a trading business and so continues.

44 *Memorandum from the Manager of El Khandaq Co-operative Union to the Director, Co-operation Department, Khartoum*, 1971, General File.

45 *Memorandum addressed to the Director, Co-operation Department, Khartoum and the Register of the Co-operative Societies dated 18.8.1972.*

# Chapter Five: Development of the Different Forms of Sharecropping

## Section I: Introduction

Ownership or control over the factors of production described in the previous chapter determines the mode of appropriation of the final product. However, ownership of these factors and the subsequent production relations based on them have experienced many changes in the last forty years or so. In this chapter the different types of share-cropping arrangements which form the basis of appropriation of surpluses, and consequently the basis of capital accumulation, will be described under different technical and social conditions. Another aim here is to see how these different arrangements have been exploited by the possessors (or controllers) of different factors, especially that of land at an earlier and capital at a later stage of development. Within the latter categories a large number of traders, some of whom had been farmers themselves, are becoming of special importance to the development of agricultural production in the area. The description here will help towards an understanding of the conditions under which the rural entrepreneurs – traders, middle peasants and migrants – were able to accumulate wealth by expropriating large surpluses from the tenant cultivators. In addition to that form of appropriation, that is through share-cropping, there are other forms of relations which suggest different modes of appropriation of surpluses. These are mainly in the government and quasi-government schemes like Burgeig and Suleim. These latter forms will be discussed in section four of this chapter.

As I have pointed out above, the changes on the technical and economic level have precipitated many changes in the social, economic and political organization of the Danagla. Among the observed changes is that of the role of the kinship group in the process of production. The tendency is towards a change from an economic organization which had been characteristically constituted in the kinship organization to one which is becoming increasingly dominated by secular values dictated by the transformation of the agricultural production from an almost totally subsistence activity into one which creates exchange values for the expanding markets. The processes involved in such development are difficult to trace beyond living memory. The *sagiya* as an irrigation technique has been in use for more than two thousand years,[1] but my description will go back only to the period shortly after the re-occupation of the Sudan by the British and Egyptians in 1899. At that time and until the Second World War the *sagiya* was the dominant means of irrigation with its particular social and economic organization until it was taken over by the spread of pump schemes and their new forms of share-cropping. This, however, does not mean the abolition of the *sagiya* as a technique of irrigation as we still find a sizeable number of them working all over the region.[2] Moreover its relations of production are still reproduced in the small and large pump schemes, particularly in the former. The persistence of the *sagiya* relations of production makes me describe the different forms of relations under both *sagiya* and the schemes as the '*sagiya* system of production'. So in the following analysis two assumptions can occur, firstly that the *sagiya* as a technique of irrigation is still at work although the social conditions of its existence are different from those forty or more years ago. Secondly, the relations of production under the *sagiya* have largely influenced the share-cropping arrangements under pump schemes, and also have virtually reproduced themselves in the increasing number of small pumps established during the period between 1955 and 1972.[3]

A scheme is suggested here for the study of the development of the *sagiya* system of production which calls for qualification from the start. The problem is to analyse the development of *sagiya* relations in isolation from other technical and social developments, and at the same time to try to establish the intricate relationships between them. Another problem of a different nature is that of the intra-regional variations which make it difficult to give an account of the whole area in respect of the introduction of innovations and their consequences in the different parts of the region. To describe the socio-economic changes influenced by a particular development of an agricultural technique, for example, presupposes its earlier impact in places where it first occurred. The importation of Egyptian Fellahin with some of their comparatively advanced agricultural equipment between 1909 and 1924 in the Suleim basin[4] had a great influence on the methods of cultivation in the areas around the basin. Although the iron plough, the *noraj* (a threshing machine) and the flail were recognized as labour-saving devices, and although they were introduced simultaneously, yet we find that the flail, unlike the other two, is unknown in some parts of the region. Moreover we can see the variations in major technical changes with the introduction and spread of power-driven pumps; they were mostly introduced into the northern part of the region first. However these present a problem less difficult than that of depicting the chronological occurrence of changes in the relations of production, the political and social organization of the Danagla. Such a situation presents the problem of making rigid periodization for the socio-economic developments in the area and their consequences in particular. A scheme is suggested here to help with the understanding of these developments and the processes underlying them.

*Phase One: before the mid-thirties* This includes the period before the 1930s, which is typical of an extensive period in the past. Apart from the gravity irrigation which started in the Suleim in the 1909, the *sagiya* was the main means of irrigation along the river banks and some parts of the Suleim basin itself. As I mentioned earlier, the social and economic organization revolved around the kinship group. As an addition to owning the land they also owned or shared the *sagiya* machine and provided most of the agricultural labour required. This form of production relations is taken as the starting point for the analysis as it is difficult to refer to previous forms of organization for lack of documented material.

*Phase Two: 1930s to 1969* During the first years of this phase the *sagiya* was dominant – until shortly after World War II when the pumps started to take over. It has been reported that the number of *sagiya* in the Northern Province was decreasing while pumps were increasing rapidly during this phase. From 9,880 *sagiya* and 240 *shadufs* in 1927, they became 6,859 and 128 in 1937, and 5,692 and 84 in 1953. The pumps increased from 63 in 1927 to 111 in 1937 and to 608 in 1953.[5] The *sagiya* was gradually giving way to modern mechanically driven pumps. But the most important feature of this phase is the persistence of the *sagiya* relations of production despite these major technical changes, and also the changes in the appropriation of the means of production.

*Phase Three: from 1970 onwards* This followed the May Revolution of 1969 when a limited land reform was implemented in Dongola region. Most of the decisions were directed to the problems of land possession, especially in the Suleim basin and co-operative schemes, share-cropping arrangements, enactment of co-operation rules, etc., which affected changes in the political and social organization of the tenant farmers.

The first two phases were characterized by minimal direct government intervention, in contrast to the central areas of the Sudan where the government had relatively more economic undertakings. Nevertheless external influences were not ruled out despite the fact that the developments characterizing the first two phases were locally induced, as Thornton noticed.[6]

In the last phase government intervention was important to the policies of distribution of land and the enactment of certain laws that guaranteed the tenants the right to cultivate, and in certain situations, to hold land for ulitization. Moreover, the co-operatives were encouraged and new legislation was made to collect the landless and tenants under viable administrative units (the co-operatives) and to allow for the acquisition of more land in the *miyri*. This last measure is different from the previous government control over land in that it allows people of limited means to share in a bigger concern whereas previously it was only open for the rich to start such projects. The importance of the government in the third phase is the pre-occupation with guaranteeing the tenant farmers better conditions of production and equitable returns and with freeing them, at least theoretically, from the domination of the local capitalists and landowners.

During these three phases one can distinguish two tendencies in the development of the Danagla economy. The first, which was more evident in the first phase, can be described as a slow process of change taking place to increase the agricultural output so as to meet the increasing demands created by the integration of the local economy with outside markets and by the fact that more consumer goods were introduced to the peasant which required more efforts to increase his surplus products. This can be accounted for by the development of the co-operative companies in the thirties which depended mainly on peasant savings and those of their migrant relatives outside. The second tendency, which prevailed in the second and third phases, is that of the increasing number of non-cultivators who had accumulated sufficient wealth from trade and other sources which enabled them to reinvest in *sagiyas* earlier, and pumps later, and to intensify their rate of accumulation of wealth and consequently the increase in surpluses appropriated from the share-cropping peasants.

These three phases will be analysed later with regard to share-cropping arrangements in the seasonal crop production which incorporate different sections of the Danagla community, which was in contrast to the share-cropping arrangements in date trees which was more or less confined to the *ahali* group.[7] The permanency of the trees coupled with their being the only cash source in the past made them highly regarded, and other non-owning groups were denied any rights of ownership in this asset as that would suggest their identification with the *ahali* group. However it was a substantial source of cash income, so that dates were very important in furnishing the *ahali* group in the past with the wherewithal to become shareholders in the co-operative companies, and to provide small pumps or *sagiyas* or the travelling costs for migrant workers to go to Egypt, Saudi Arabia or the Gulf Emirates.

The seasonal crops, on the other hand, were until recently grown for food requirements, and all the social groups of the Danagla were involved, either by providing the land and irrigation (separately and combined) or by expending their direct labour as share-cropping tenants. In the last category we find that all groups are represented whereas it is evident that the non-owners of date trees and land had very slim chances of being represented in the first category.[8] So there is a clear difference between the ownership of land and capital, and labour. The first two (especially land) were mostly owned by the *ahali*, except for those members of this who were alienated from their land before the end of the last century.[9] This contributed to the emergence of a class of landless *ahali* who could only survive by being share-croppers with the land-owning class. The division, then, lies between the class owning land in the *milk* from within the *ahali* and a socially and ethnically heterogeneous class of landless tenants and share-croppers. In the past the ownership of land had ascendancy over the other factors of production but gradually this situation started to change to give ascendancy to capital when investment became possible in modern irrigational techniques and in the extension of cultivable land in the *miyri*.

## Section II: Share-cropping of Dates

At present there is less share-cropping in dates than there was because of the lack of unoccupied *milk* land, and because those who can acquire rights in *miyri* land are sufficiently wealthy to plant their own date trees.[10] However, share-cropping in this main source of cash provided land for the landless to grow trees on; and also the necessary costs for the land-owning poor and women to share the benefits of the date crop. Previously it was impossible to grow permanent crops in the *miyri* land and that in a way set a legal restriction on who could own date trees and by definition that meant the *milk* land-owners. Non-owners of *milk* land were able to share in the distribution of dates, and consequently had a continuous cash income through share-cropping.

The shares in the date crop basically accrue to the providers of three different factors; the land to grow the trees; the shoots which used to be brought from outside the area and required a suitable amount of ready money; and the watering of the shoots until they reach a certain stage which takes between three and four years. Watering then demanded much effort as the trees were usually planted on high ground which the *sagiya* would not irrigate.

The ideal situation was to provide the three factors and be entitled to the whole product of the trees. This meant that one would have to be from among the *milk* land-owners, owning or sharing a *sagiya*, and have sufficient wealth to provide one's own shoots or use hired labour for the manual work of digging and wall-building and fence-making.[11] Alternatively the land-owner could rely on others to provide the shoots while he provides the necessary labour or entrusts the latter task to a third person to provide watering which used to be by carrying water in pots from the river or wells. So for share-cropping in dates we find that there are three partners (or elements) to the relationship, the land owner, the shoot provider and the one who undertakes the watering. Each of these partners is entitled to one-third of the crop with slight variations here and there. However, the system of distribution of the date tree product is very simple if the situation remains as it had been at the time of planting the tree. Complications ensue over inheritance rights, partial sale of a tree, or the division of by-products such as the leaves, the trunk if it has fallen, and so on, and settlement of these sometimes requires the mediation of the village head or other people.

These shares differ depending on the mode of provision of each factor. In many cases one share disappears as people have started to root their own shoots or buy them. The correct method of rooting shoots is important for lessening the risk that the shoot might never develop. The method used reflects on the price of the shoot and sometimes on the share accorded to it. For example, a new method depends on secondary rooting of a shoot in a tin full of earth; it is separated from the mother tree after sufficient roots have grown, the tin is then cut and the shoot planted in its final station. This method is more valuable than that of simply separating them from the mother tree and planting them so that they will root by themselves. Again, the variations in land shares differ with the ease of watering the trees and also the suitability of land for the production of other crops. If watering is easy the share for it may be just one-fifth of the crop, and on sandy land, which means building of walls, the land may also have a fifth or at the best a quarter. If the land-owner prepares the land and digs a well for watering, then he might hire a wage labourer to water the shoots; or give a fifth of the crop for another person to do the job.

So this date tree share-cropping arrangement tends to give the landless rich and landless poor access to land as both can provide what they can of the factors of production: the rich the costs of the shoots, preparation of land and digging of a well if necessary; and the poor the watering if water has to be drawn from a well or be carried in pots from the river. At present there is no change in the distribution of date crops whose trees have initially been grown under such an arrangement as it still follows the one-third pattern of distribution for each factor in the production. However there are changes in distribution, but not in the shares of the different factors of production, and also in the basic method of date production as individuals have started growing their own date trees. The changes in the distribution do not really contradict the one-third arrangement but work within this arrangement itself. They mainly arise from the Islamic law of inheritance, and from the sale of parts or shares of date trees.

To elaborate on this point, I think it would be of interest to quote at length a 'Land Settlement' officer in charge of the census of date trees in 1919, which to a large extent depicts the method of distribution today. He wrote:

> The question naturally arises 'How can a date tree be divided up into parts or what is the use to a man of owning say $\frac{3}{16}$ of an indivisible entity, like a date tree?' The explanation is simple. The principle comes into practical application only when the crop is gathered, and it is the fruit that is divided up each year among several owners. Even when, as will be seen later, there are several trees subject to the most complicated cross-division of different partners, the registration of which entails elaborate mathematical calculations to arrive at the proper fractions or indeed often becomes impossible, there is no real difficulty in the division of the dates – which is easily carried out without any knowledge of mathematical formulae. The dates of five trees in a single clump, for instance, are collected into heaps. The first division is probably into three heaps representing the three equal shares of the original owners. One of these thirds is possibly owned now by several heirs of the original owner, and it may be necessary to divide this heap into elevenths. Moh. Ahmed, one of them, takes his share which is two of these small heaps and goes off with it. Meanwhile the fruit of another tree of which he owns $\frac{1}{2}$ has been collected and put in a separate heap for him – and he takes this off and pours it into his own separate individual heap, and so on for all the trees in which he has a share. At the end he has all the dates he is entitled to from different trees collected in one heap, and he has never had to trouble his mind in the least as to the working out of the sum $2/11$ of $\frac{1}{3}$ of $5 + \frac{1}{8} + 1/5$ of $\frac{1}{2}$ of 7 or whatever it may be. The registration of his ownership is a different thing . . . [12]

The situation described by Leach depicts the final result of the complications resulting from inheritance or purchase. As I have shown earlier, the *milk* land and the date trees on it were not to be sold even within the kinship group. But the disgrace of selling a part or a share in date trees can be accepted. So we can imagine a man who bought one-sixth of a date tree in *sagiya* A, has one-third of two others in *sagiya* B which he has bought, and one-sixteenth of three trees in *sagiya* C which he had inherited from his father. If this man dies leaving seven children, three of whom are daughters, then the division by the heaping procedure will be as follows. In the first *sagiya* A, the product of the tree will be put in six heaps and the heirs will take one and put it aside. Then the crop of the two trees in *sagiya* B will be put in three heaps and the heirs will take one and put it in the first heap. Then the share (one-sixteenth) in the three trees in *sagiya* C is brought and added to the previous shares. At the point of collecting all their shares the share-cropping arrangements end, and the distribution becomes one of inheritance in which the Islamic laws operate. Now each son is entitled to twice the share of a sister. So the whole lot is divided into eleven heaps so that every son takes two heaps and the daughters take one heap each.

As I pointed out at the beginning of the chapter, share-cropping in date trees provided most of the villagers with a permanent source of cash to meet the requirements of land taxes, the purchase of consumer goods and the financial costs of some of their social occasions, like marriages, circumcisions, pilgrimage, etc.

In addition to the owners of the factors of production who are mainly from the *ahali* group, other non-*ahali*, that is the Sudaniyya and Arabs, have their shares in the date crop. Also we find other claims especially those of the government and the headman of the villages. The government tax has always been in cash from the owners of date trees but the most important tax here is that levied on the non-owners from their share of dates which they acquired by providing different kinds of labour. Those who cross-pollinate the trees and cut the bunches at harvest (mostly Arabs or Manasir from further south), are entitled to one bunch[13] from every tree they pollinate and cut. The tax on this goes to the *samad* of the *sagiya* concerned and to the *shaykh* of the village. The *samad* takes one half of the bunch and then divides that between himself and the *shaykh*, allowing the pollinating and cutting labour one half of the bunch. The dependence of some Arabs on date cross-pollination and cutting for particular *ahali* owners adds to the strengthening of the patron-client-type relationship obtaining in the seasonal share-cropping. An Arab would agree to work as a *jiygol* (combined agricultural labourer and domestic servant), and at the same time pollinate his patron's date trees and be entitled to a half bunch in every tree.

Others can also obtain shares by providing collecting labour at harvest time. People move from one *sagiya* to another helping with the collection of scattered dates. At the end of each 'cutting' each is given four to ten handfuls of dates (depending on their age and how long they have been engaged in collection) and by the end of the day they return home with a considerable number of dates. Although the shares of these are not comparable with those of the owners of the date trees, yet this provides them with cash like the rest of the villagers. It is apparent then how the date tree is important not only to the owners but also to non-owners in providing cash income. It was especially so in the past when there were no other cash sources within the area except what was sent back by migrants, who could not have travelled in the first place unless they had cash to travel with and to a large extent that had been furnished by the cash returns of the date trees.

Date share-cropping then has had two effects – one the provision of cash for almost all the population through the systems of reward described above, and the other the provision of a channel of investment for local entrepreneurs who had accumulated wealth in agriculture, in trade, or from savings in exile as emigrants. Traders have been the most equipped with cash in the villages and have wide contacts outside. Their knowledge of trader friends in the Mahas and Shaiqiya regions who could facilitate the provision of shoots, or act as hosts if the trader himself was travelling, gave them an advantage over other relatively wealthy peasants who could at least afford the land or the irrigation. So it was always the practice that the traders, in addition to what they planted in their land, also provided a large number of land-owners with shoots and became entitled to one-third for that. Suleiman Khalid, a crop merchant of Mushu, has date trees in the 25 *sagiyas* constituting the village land.[14] He declined to give the exact number of trees or their yield, but in the register he holds a little over 400 trees. That does not mean he totally possesses these trees, nor can I say how many other shares he has got in trees registered in others' names,[15] but what is registered in his name shows him as the biggest owner in the village. This shows how the traders can extend their activities by transferring their capital from one sphere to the other and using it in the opportunities open within the local economy. An important constraint on the traders, though, was the restrictions on growing date trees in *milk* land. But this situation is now changing as those who are able financially can have their own orchards on *miyri* land and direct investments in agriculture without necessarily going through the complicated arrangement of share-cropping.

**Section III: Share-cropping of Seasonal Crops**[15]

The importance of share-cropping in seasonal crops derives from the fact that they reflect, by the way they are distributed, the significance of the different forces of production to the Danagla on the one hand, and the relationships between the people participating in the production process on the other. Moreover, the production of seasonal crops brings the different social classes in the villages into relationships different from those obtaining in the share-cropping of dates. Relations of dependency, which are to some extent found in the date share-cropping arrangements, are to be contrasted with the relations of conflict which characterize the types of arrangement with seasonal crops. The development and changes in these relations have been constrained by the particular stage of development of the forces of production and the relations of production prevailing at any particular time. An attempt is made here to see the developments in property relations and in the relations of production; and how these influence the relationship between the different social groups constituting the Danagla community. However, the changes in the forces are more discernible than those in the relations of production. Yet they depict a tendency towards the development of a social structure based on alliances of class rather than on ethnic and tribal affiliations. This tendency is clearly manifested in certain parts of the region and in a specific type of agriculture particularly that practised by local traders and other entrepreneurs. The application of the last tendency is then limited and no general conclusion can be based on it. However it represents an extreme form of development that the production process is approaching. Still we find that the relations of production which were prevailing in the twenties remain dominant even after the radical changes experienced by the forces of production described in the last chapter. So it is expected that we can find different forms of production co-existing which can be distinguished by an elaborate description of the production process and the modes of appropriation and distribution of products.

a. Phase I The *sagiya* System.

The *sagiya* was a radical development from the earlier means of irrigation, like the *shaduf* (a hand-operated lever for raising water), in that it combined human and animal energy whereas the *shaduf* depended only on human energy. It is more efficient in raising water yet technically when compared with the modern irrigational pumps it is inefficient. D. J. Shaw has shown its inefficiency in four ways: firstly, there is the loss of water from spillage; secondly, there is the high resistance of wood friction; thirdly, half of the land cultivated should be under fodder to feed the draught animals; and finally, it requires cheap labour which is unavailable.[16] However, these shortcomings were matched by the relatively low costs of making and installing a *sagiya*, and also its building and operating depended totally on local resources. Bond described how it was easy to make and install a *sagiya*:

> In a few hours a man and a few boys will turn a jumble of logs and rope like a gigantic jackdaw's nest into a working *sagiya*. It is built on mud against the face of a crumbling cliff of earth, subject to erosion by river action at various levels, it has to bear a heavy and oscillating load for months on end, and has to rely for stability on gravity, friction and string.[17]

However simply described, *sagiya*-making involved skilled carpentry which was provided by a few experts in the area. Also the building of *sagiya* was not only the assembly of a 'jumble of logs', but the right logs, the expert craftsman, and so on (see Plate 6). What added to its cost was the animals, which were rare and comparatively expensive in the area, and that was reflected in the large share of the animals in the crops (about 50 per cent). An example (unrepresentative as it is only 0.6 faddan) is of a working *sagiya* in Akkad. The cost of that *sagiya* being newly erected at the time of my visit (April 1977) was as follows: £S46 was paid for the *dulab* (the wood and its carpentry), and £S1.50mm for the ferry boat which brought it from the carpenter's place. He also paid one pound for the pots, and he made his own ropes. That makes the cost, apart from that of the animals at £S48. 50mm.[18] £S85 was paid for one cow, which was also a milch cow. The other cow used was borrowed from a friend, who kept it as a milch cow, in exchange for its fodder. The six *kasr*[19] under cultivation were all under vegetables as the owner was himself a tenant farmer with the pump scheme and from his tenancy there he provided the fodder for the cows. So in this situation, the cost of installing a *sagiya* in money terms is higher than it was. The same *sagiya* owner told me that the machine and the cow together would not have cost him more than £S30 in the past. Until the 1930s this meant a large sum of money very few people could provide.

The importance of the *sagiya* in production is decreasing and pumps are progressively taking over. However at present no figures of the number of *sagiyas* (except for the Suleim, see p.150) are available though estimates of the areas cultivated by the *sagiyas* are kept in the regional Agricultural Office. These show a steady decrease in the years 1967/8 to 1971/72, despite the fact that in 1972–74 the areas under *sagiya* cultivation showed a considerable increase (see Table VII). The concentration of *sagiyas* seemed to be in the islands and on small plots of land which can be useful only for vegetables and other cash crops which are either not allowed in the schemes or not grown on large areas of land. In the years 1972/73 and 1973/74 more onions, cumin, garlic and peas were cultivated in the *sagiyas*.[20]

**Table VII Comparison Between Areas Cultivated by *sagiyas* and Pumps 1964/1974**

| Year Two Seasons | Areas under pumps | Areas under *sagiyas* | Total | % pump | % *sagiya* | No. of pumps |
|---|---|---|---|---|---|---|
| 1964/65 | 31,476 | 6,260 | 37,736 | 83.4 | 16.6 | 279 |
| 1965/66 | 31,960 | 5,231 | 37,191 | 85.0 | 14.0 | 305 |
| 1966/67 | 32,932 | 6,599 | 39,531 | 83.0 | 17.0 | 329 |
| 1967/68 | 34,988 | 3,954 | 38,942 | 90.0 | 10.0 | 377 |
| 1968/69 | 28,996 | 4,924 | 33,920 | 85.5 | 14.5 | 406 |
| 1969/70 | 34,075 | 3,706 | 37,781 | 90.2 | 9.8 | 315 |
| 1970/71 | 33,563 | 4,547 | 38,110 | 88.0 | 12.0 | — |
| 1971/72 | 34,090 | 4,311 | 38,401 | 87.0 | 13.0 | — |
| 1972/73 | 30,623 | 8,061 | 38,684 | 79.0 | 21.0 | 466 |
| 1973/74 | 35,024 | 9,210 | 44,234 | 79.0 | 21.0 | 466 |

## Crop Distribution Under the *sagiya* System

There used to be different methods of crop distribution depending on the type of crops, the season of the year, the nature of land (and in some cases its type), and the relationship between the people participating in *sagiya* production. These variations attracted the attention of agricultural economists like Shaw, as he writes: 'The feature of *sagiya* cultivation . . . was the partnership arrangements which developed between the parties supplying the various inputs required. Partnership varied from one place to the next.'[21]

Despite the variations mentioned we find that the general rule of distribution was that the animals, whose ownership was not necessarily specific took half of the product. The other half went to the other factors of production – the *sagiya*, land and labour. In most cases the *tarabla* were expected to provide half of the animals required, in other words they supplied a part of the capital invested in the *sagiya*. The final distribution usually took the following pattern with slight variations:[22]

| | No. of *khushum* | % of total |
|---|---|---|
| *sagiya* | 1 *khashm* | 8.3 |
| animals | 6 *khushum* | 50.0 |
| *aurwatti* | 1 *khashm* | 8.3 |
| *samad moiya* | 1 *khashm* | 8.3 |
| *tarabla* | 3 *khushum* | 25.0 |

The shares shown above are not different from those described by Nicholls and Shaw. But Nicholls seemed to sum the *tarabla* shares and that of half the animals together as the *tarabla* usually provided half of the animals. It was almost always so, but there were instances when some *tarabla* did not supply any animals. Moreover I separated the two to show how irrigation used to appropriate (as it still does) most of the cultivators' products.[23] Two chances were open to the *tarabla* to increase their share in their products, that was by providing half of the animals required (at least eight), and by using their children to work as drivers. So the maximum share in the crop one could obtain depended on the provision of half the animals and the driver. By so doing one could take up to seven *khushum* if one cultivated one's own land, and without the co-operation of another *turbal*. That rarely took place as it was against the interest of the *samad* who mainly depended on appropriating up to half of the products by investing in the *sagiya* animals and the driver. His supervisory function entitled him to more *khushum* if he provided the *sagiya*, half or more of the animals, land or part of it, and the driver. The total income for the *samad* depended on how he could realize and exploit these opportunities and basically on his reputation, his mental and financial capabilities.[24] If he did not own either the *sagiya* or the land he should be known as an experienced and trustworthy farmer and consequently would be able to rent them from those who owned them. He might provide a *jiygol* as a *turbal* and appropriate his share in the crops too.

As to the organization of work in the *sagiya*, the duties of the *samad* were twofold; one concerning the running and maintaining of the *sagiya* and the main irrigational canal, *al-gadwal al-dakkar*, and the other concerning the agricultural operations like clearing, preparation, sowing, etc. In both he would take the tasks which needed special experience while leaving the others for the *tarabla*. His work in the *sagiya* was mainly administrative; supervising the condition and working of the machine, the preparation of the small irrigation basins and the clearing of the main channels to and from the *sagiya*. He also arranged for the *faza'a* at harvest with his *tarabla* sharing the expenses of food and drinks provided for the work party. On the other hand his *tarabla* provided the rest of the agricultural work with some help from the *samad* who also took a *turbal*'s share.

*Development of property relations under the sagiya system* The system of distribution which was dominant before the mid-thirties has hardly experienced any changes except for minor variations referred to earlier when share-cropping was used; that is the shares remained the same for the different factors of production. However, different systems of *sagiya* cultivation emerged ranging from one which depended totally on the kinship group (see Chapter 3) to one where totally hired labour was used.

The variations in the property relations would suggest one or more of the following situations. These, however, do not logically follow one another but coexist in different combinations with one situation (situation 'C' below) being present in the four situations. The distinctive feature will then be the property in land and *sagiya* (both the machine and the animals) which can be used to depict the different developments in the *sagiya* system.

## Situation A

The ownership of factors of production was as follows, taken from the standpoint of the man who actually undertook agriculture as an occupation.[25]

| *Land* | *sagiya* | *animals* | *family labour* | *hired labour* | *turbal* |
|---|---|---|---|---|---|
| + | + | + | + | + | — |

This situation represents the extreme which was hardly ever worked in the period under study. The peasant here is self-sufficient in almost everything except that he might use hired labour or *faza'a*. This corresponds to the conditions described in Chapter Three when the economic organization was mainly constituted in the kinship system.

**Situation B**

| Land | sagiya | animals | family hired labour | labour | turbal |
|---|---|---|---|---|---|
| + | + | + | + | + | — |

In this situation there was always the shortage of land in one *sagiya*. Usually there was a partnership in the machine or a man might hire it from a neighbour and pay the rent for it. Otherwise he might incorporate his small plot in the established *sagiya* and be entitled to his land rent, his labour reward and animal share if he provided them or part of them. However land rent alone could not be a large source of income unless one owned a number of plots, which was unusual especially when we refer to the situation in the *milk* land. As to the labour resources they were not different from the first situation (A).

**Situation C**

| Land | sagiya | animals | family hired labour | labour | turbal |
|---|---|---|---|---|---|
| + | + | ± | — | + | + |

This is the situation where peasants were able to invest in land and *sagiya* and practise share-cropping. It is this development that has made it possible for the relatively wealthy peasants to accumulate capital for further investments. The combination of the ownership of land and means of irrigation allowed some of the middle peasants to appropriate the surplus labour of fellow peasant – *tarabla*. This was possible when larger areas of land were put under cultivation and larger areas were annexed to the *sagiya* land from the *miyri*.

In this situation the main characteristic was the withdrawal of the *samad* from direct involvement in cultivation (as used to be the case in situations 'A' and 'B'). There was then a change of personnel in the *tarabla* and *samdas* who could be non-owners in the land or the *sagiya*, and under this situation the *tarabla* might not provide any of the animals. The local description 'a cultivator with his hoe only' was used for the class of *tarabla* in this situation which coincided with the beginning of the thirties and the horizontal expansion of cultivable land in the *miyri*. Here the former agricultural labourers and the Sudaniyya assumed the *tarabla* status especially when the ex-slaves were encouraged to stay by being formally given (by the ex-masters) their freedom and the right to cultivate in the masters' *sagiya*. The impact of this mobility was great as it allowed the poor and the landless to start cultivation in two ways: either as share-croppers, as with the landless poor *ahali*, the Sudaniyya and the settling Arab nomads; or as investors, especially when *matarat* started to develop, as with those who were able to afford to build *sagiya*, reclaim land and provide the necessary animals. This last group came mainly from the middle peasant class, or from outside the agricultural sector. Under this situation the kinship group and the immediate family was removed further from the production process, especially when access to the *miyri* was open to whoever could provide the necessary expenses.

The relationships characteristic of this situation have been present for a long time, indeed until the present even after the introduction of pumps and the incorporation of *miyri* land and the limited reforms mentioned in the previous chapter concerning land and production relations.

**Situation D**

Only hired labour used.

In this situation all the factors of production except labour were owned, or in the case of land held, by a wealthy entrepreneur. This started simultaneously with situation 'C', i.e., when investment was allowed in the *miyri*. Production here depended totally on hired labour and no share-cropping arrangements were used. This was a suitable channel of investment for the town traders who started *matarat* as vegetable and other cash-crop gardens. The hired labour was rewarded in cash and in some cases the worker was allowed to cultivate a small plot for his vegetable needs which in one way or another constituted a part of his wage as it was usually included in the initial work agreement.

However situation 'D' represents the highest degree of development the *sagiya* system has attained, and it is now becoming used largely in small pumps either on *matarat* or from the river. But it is not widespread, and the system used more commonly is still that of situation 'C' in one form or another. In the following sections I will try to show how the changes in the position of the cultivators of situation 'C' took place, and their consequences.

b. Phase II. Under Pump Schemes Until 1969

This is the period when most of the developments in the productive forces and the relations of production occurred. These have been neither even nor stable as we find that different forms of production relations obtained and also movements from new forms to older ones, especially after the development of small individual pumps at the end of the fifties. Before then the area was irrigated by relatively large schemes in the big co-operative companies and private pump schemes.

For the purpose of analysing the development in the irrigation techniques, which presuppose the expansion of agricultural production both horizontally and vertically, we can distinguish two patterns which had, in various ways, influenced the relations of production. Firstly, there were the co-operative companies and the individual and partnership schemes which started shortly after the First World War, and which initiated radical changes in the production process yet utilized the former organization and the relations of the *sagiya*. However, the *sagiya* system did not last for long as it was, but became modified to suit the new requirements of production. The most striking change in organization was the introduction of the 'tenancy holder' to cope with the new situation arising from the increasing financial and credit needs which were beyond the *tarabla*'s capabilities. This continued to be the case, with this intermediary, until the beginning of the fifties when the co-operation regulations were applied effectively in the co-operative societies and gradually had their influence on private, individual and partnership in the area. The second pattern was the development of the small pumps owned by individuals or partnerships in the late fifties. Along the Nile banks the small pumps took a different course of development from those on the Suleim basin as the latter, except for very few, were installed individually by wealthy people for the production of cash crops using different types of share-cropping arrangements from those on the river. Many of these small pumps were installed to replace the *sagiya* as a technique of irrigation, nevertheless they preserved the *sagiya* economic and social organization described earlier. They were mostly run on one or more of the situations described at the end of the previous section.

We have, then, two main courses of development with particular variations in each of the two. In the big schemes we find slight variations in the relations of production arising from the legal status of the individual schemes and from the types of land incorporated in them. However, some of the small pumps can be classified with these with respect to their relations of production but many of them differ from the big schemes and more or less resemble the *sagiya* organization in various aspects. The exceptions are those of the Suleim basin which were individually-owned either by the peasants themselves or obtained through a system of mortgage which allowed the creditor to virtually own the pump though not registered in his name.

From the introduction of the big schemes there followed two significant consequences. The first one was the expansion of cultivable land to the extent that the existing labour resources were insufficient to cope with the increasing areas. A large number of the nomadic tribes in the desert, who used to come down to the villages to work during harvest seasons as hired labour for short periods,[26] were able to settle and supplied their labour on a more regular basis especially when diversification of crops started in 1945. Gradually most of them assumed the positions of *tarabla*, a development which led some of the former *ahali* who worked as *tarabla* to seek employment outside, and to the creation of a new farming class of share-croppers drawing from the *ahali*, the Sudaniyya and the Arabs: a heterogenous class made up from the different tribal and ethnic groups in the area. The second consequence was in the organization and administration of farm work. Those who started the schemes were allocated tenancies in them as tenants responsible for the supervision of the farmers' work, and were answerable to the scheme board in all matters concerning the running of the tenancy. On his side this tenancy holder was responsible, in addition to the farmers' work, also for the provision of the financial requirements of the tenancy and credit facilities for his farmers when needed. This was important in creating a dependency relationship between the *tarabla* and the tenancy holder who should be in a sound financial position and capable of providing cash whenever needed.

Although the tenancy holder resembled the *samad moiya* in the representation aspect, yet he was different in that his share in production was larger than that of the former. In this phase the tenancy combined both the representation of the land-owners (in the case of scheme controllers), and the supervisory role of the *samad moiya*. His role was disguised as the owner of the tenancy and consequently he appropriated the share of land in addition to the share accruing to his services to the scheme and the farmers alike. So we have this tenancy holder as the most distinguishing characteristic of this phase. He acted like the *samad moiya* under the *sagiya* system as an entrepreneur using both his financial resources and administrative skills to run the tenancy on behalf of the scheme. At the final distribution he was entitled to one quarter of the total produce as reward. Actually he provided all the requirements for the tenancy which was a small part of a larger unit (the scheme) in which he had a vested interest as a shareholder, and by so doing the wealthy people of the area were able to appropriate a larger portion of the *tarabla*'s surplus products through the shares accruing to their administrative and financial functions and also from dividends from the profits of the scheme.

So it was the control of irrigation and land (not necessarily its absolute ownership) that gave some of the wealthy *ahali* and later other wealthy entrepreneurs the opportunity to exploit these sub-tenant cultivators both economically and politically. The relationship of the *tarabla*/capitalists has been referred to in the previous chapter but a point is worth mentioning here. It was not the scarcity of land, as was thought by Adam[27] that led to that form of production relations, rather, I think the explanation can be found in the way these local capitalists are trying to have the maximum profits from their investment in agriculture. To accomplish that two concepts were utilized. The first was to consider and treat the *miyri* land as if it was *milk* and demand the rent on it; and the second was to preserve, or at least not to disturb, the *sagiya* relations of production which allowed for more share in production to go for irrigation. It is quite evident that the *tarabla* accepted that system of share-cropping because the absolute quantities of crops accruing to them are larger than those under *sagiya* cultivation. Moreover, the *tarabla* had to expend comparatively less labour as a result of the use of machinery both in irrigation and in most of the agricultural operations. In relative terms they were more exploited than they had been under the *sagiya* since under the *sagiya* they had been able to invest also by providing half of the draught animals for the working of the *sagiya*.

Under this phase which extended from the mid-thirties until the beginning of the seventies, when political action was taken to change the relations of production to benefit the actual cultivators, the system of distribution was as follows:

| | | |
|---|---|---|
| the scheme | 6 *khushum* | 50 per cent |
| tenancy holder | 3 *khushum* | 25 per cent |
| *tarabla* | 3 *khushum* | 25 per cent |

In comparing this distribution with that of the *sagiya* it is apparent that there was no fundamental change in the basis of distribution nor in the shares accruing to the labour. But it is clear that the shares of capital and land are becoming larger and furnishing the owners (controllers) with more income than they had under the *sagiya* system of cultivation.

c. Phase III. Under Pump Schemes from 1970

This phase differs from phase II in two respects: namely, the greater expansion by agricultural schemes in the *miyri* land; and the observable changes in the relations of production and the share-cropping arrangements induced by government action. Within this phase I will describe two other forms of production relations in the area which follow different patterns from the one obtaining in the private schemes, viz., those on the Suleim basin and the Burgeig government schemes. Both of these schemes started many years ago (Suleim in 1909 and Burgeig 1944), yet they were not included in the analysis in the previous phases of development because they are more or less governmentally sponsored and have different sets of production relations. The small pumps are not important for the analysis of the production relations as they reproduced in different forms the *sagiya* system. In the Suleim, however, the small pumps are different and will be described later on as they reflect clearly the extent of traders' and other entrepreneurs' involvement in agriculture and their different usurious activities. The resolutions of 1969 were mainly directed towards abolishing this involvement in the Suleim and in the co-operative schemes in the area which more or less fell below government expectations.

Although co-operatives started earlier in the area yet the implementation of the co-operation regulations had been effected in various ways and at different times after the 1948 co-operation ordinance. During the period 1954 to 1959 a number of co-operative schemes started to abide by the principle of the half-sharing of the products after the deduction of the costs of shared operations, a principle which was not obligatory to other non-co-operative schemes in the region. The influence of this was significant especially in places where a co-operative scheme, for example, was within the vicinity of another company or individual scheme. In a period of acute shortage of agricultural labour, due to massive waves of emigration in the period following independence in 1956, competition was high for the recruitment of *tarabla*. With the elimination of the tenancy holders[28] in the co-operatives, a drift towards the co-operative schemes from other schemes started which caused other residual problems for the co-operatives, eg, overcrowding, and hence smaller returns for the schemes and the individual tenants. Nevertheless, this movement of tenants forced some of the companies and individual schemes to change their systems of share-cropping and drop the tenancy holder and so approximate to the system of distribution in the co-operatives.

The pace of change was intensified in 1969 when the President of the State visited the area and a number of resolutions were passed concerning the position of *tarabla* and tenants, co-operative schemes and land possession. One of the first resolutions was to give full support and assistance to co-operative schemes from the government, and to the transformation of company and individual schemes into co-operative schemes when their pumping licences expired. This resolution never came into effect but it precipitated important consequences when it was passed.[29]

Moreover, the co-operatives were given priority in utilizing *miyri* land and in access to loans from the Agricultural Bank. The second major resolution was the declaration 'The land for the tiller' which was mainly directed to the appropriation of land in the Suleim basin to the peasants who used to be involved in a different web of production and credit relations with the local traders and other entrepreneurs. The impact of these resolutions was different for different schemes as well as in different settings. In situations where land could be extended for the co-operatives it was evident that the consequences for the relations of production were significant. The competition for the limited number of *tarabla* within a village or its neighbourhood forced the schemes with tenancy holders to follow the co-operative pattern of distribution whereby the product was divided in the ratio of 1:1 between the scheme and the tenant farmer after the deduction of shared costs. This pattern at present predominates in almost all the big river-bank schemes and the Letti basin schemes in the south. Another factor is the limitation on the extension of land within islands where land is almost totally *milk*. The Bediyn Agricultural Company, for example, until 1977 retained the tenancy holder because of the land limitation, and the fact that it was wholly on *milk* land which made it difficult for the authorities to enforce any restriction or change on it.[30]

Other cases arise from the different land types and the legal status of the schemes. The two examples below (Case I and Case II) can illustrate my point.

Case I: Barakoal Agricultural Company

This is a private company with the shareholders mostly from the Bedayriyya traders centred in Amintego (a nearby market centre) and the land under cultivation is totally *miryi* in the Letti basin. Until 1977, the land of this scheme was not fully utilized and reclamation of more land was under way, and this required more capital inputs. So financial sources were required for clearing and levelling the land – a situation which called for the retaining of the tenancy holder of phase II but with a little difference. There are different arrangements between the tenancy holder and his *tarabla* which are different from those between the scheme and the *tarabla* because of the arrangement that all the claims of the tenancy holder fall on the cultivators' share. In this scheme there are four different arrangements:

1. the tenancy holder levels the land, pays the land tax (10 piastres per *faddan*), provides fertilizers and credit for the *tarabla* in the pre-harvest period. At harvest he takes one-twelfth of the share of the scheme and one-third of that of the *tarabla*; or
2. the holder undertakes the clearing and levelling of land only and he is entitled to one-eighth of the *tarabla*'s share; or
3. when the land had already been under use, then one-twelfth of the *tarabla*'s share goes to the tenancy holder as land rent and the former undertake all other responsibilities; or
4. the tenancy holder pays the land tax and is entitled to one-quarter of the *tarabla*'s share. This is not common, in fact only one case was reported in the scheme where the *tarabla* were newcomers to it.

It must be mentioned that if this was a co-operative, land would have no rent as the tax is usually paid by the licensee, and in this case the scheme. Here *miyri* land is accorded *milk* land status just by the right of reclamation. In this scheme if we assume the total production of one tenancy as twenty volume units of grain (say *ardabs*), then the final distribution will look as follows in the four different situations (Table VIII).

**Table VIII**
**Crop Distribution in Barakoal Scheme**

| Situation | Scheme share | % | *tarabla* share | % | tenancy holder share | % |
|---|---|---|---|---|---|---|
| 1 | 9.17 | 45.9 | 6.67 | 33.3 | 4.16 | 20.8 |
| 2 | 10.0 | 50.0 | 8.75 | 43.75 | 1.25 | 6.25 |
| 3 | 10.0 | 50.0 | 9.17 | 45.8 | 0.83 | 4.2 |
| 4 | 10.0 | 50.0 | 7.5 | 37.5 | 2.5 | 12.5 |

Case II: Shaykh-Shariyf South Co-operative Scheme
The difference in this co-operative comes from the fact that *miyri* land is accorded the status of *milk* land, not through reclamation right as in Barakoal, but by a legal principle, *hag al-gusad* (right of frontage) which gives the owners of *milk* land the priority in access to the *miyri* (*gusad*) facing their land. This *gusad* land is accorded freehold status and land rent is claimed from it. Another difference here is when the tenant cultivates his own land (both *milk* and *gusad*). He is then entitled to one-twelfth of his product in his *milk* land as rent but does not pay any rent or tax for the *gusad* land as that will be paid by the scheme, nor is he entitled to land rent from it. If he gives his land to a tenant cultivator then the latter has to pay one-eighth of his share in the *gusad* land to the land-owner, and one-twelfth of the total product of the *milk* land. So in both situations (whether the land-owner cultivates himself or leases his land), the distribution will be as follows, assuming that half of the land is *milk* and half is *gusad* with similar productivity, and that the production is twenty units of grain in both the lands.

*Situation I*: Owner cultivating himself:

| | | |
|---|---|---|
| Owner-cultivator' share | 10.42 units | 52 per cent |
| Scheme's shares | 9.58 units | 48 per cent |

*Situation II:* Owner leasing land to a turbal:

| | | |
|---|---|---|
| Land-owner's share | 1.45 units | 7.25 per cent |
| Scheme's share | 9.58 units | 47.9 per cent |
| turbal's share | 8.96 units | 44.8 per cent |

These two cases (Case I and Case II) show the extent of variation in the share-cropping in the area generally, even within the same scheme, depending on the availability of tenancies on the one hand, and the suitability of the land for cultivation as well as the presence of other competitive schemes in the vicinity.

However the distribution of crops in almost all schemes seems to follow a general pattern whereby the product is divided into two halves after the deduction of land rent, if it is *milk*, the costs of seeds, ploughing, fertilizers and threshing exenses. The development of the systems of distribution and property relations can be summed up in the following table (Table IX), assuming, again, a hypothetical situation of fixed area of land and constant productivity of twenty units which in percentage form shows the changes in the distribution of crops under the three different phases of agricultural development. Nevertheless, we have to bear in mind that the productivity of land has changed as well as the fertility of land brought under use, and this is reflected in the quantity of grain produced per *faddan*. The annexed *miyri* is less productive than the *milk*, but that shortcoming has been compensated for by horizontal expansion. But what is really important here are the changes in the *tarabla* shares from the *sagiya* phase when irrigation demanded up to 60 per cent of their product, and also in the land rent which is showing a considerable decrease as more *miryi* is incorporated.[31]

**Table IX* Crop Distribution under the Sagiya and Pump Schemes (Phase I and II)**

| | | *sagiya* | Animals | Aurwatti (driver) | *samad moiya* | Scheme | *nimra* holder | *tarabla* |
|---|---|---|---|---|---|---|---|---|
| SAGIYA | share | 1.66 | 10 | 1.66 | 1.66 | — | — | 5 |
| | % | 8.3 | 50.0 | 8.3 | 8.3 | — | — | 25.0 |
| SCHEME PHASE I | share | — | — | — | — | 6 | 3 | 3 0 |
| | % | — | — | — | — | 50.0 | 25.0 | 25.0 |
| SCHEME PHASE II | share | — | — | — | — | — | 6 | 65 |
| | % | — | — | — | — | — | 50.0 | 50.0 |

* Division takes place after deducting land rent (when land is *milk* land) and seeds, and under phase II of the schemes, the costs of ploughing, fertilizers and threshing.

Under the schemes phase II, we find that although the tenant cultivators had the same ratio as under the *sagiya* system yet their chances of increasing their shares are less because under the *sagiya* they could provide up to half of the animals and be entitled to an extra 25 per cent, or provide a driver who might be a child or a younger brother and also be entitled to one extra share. However under this situation the tenants' shares were exclusively for their human labour and there was no chance of investment in animals or a driver. The animals were used then to help in other agricultural tasks formerly performed by human beings like hoeing and threshing which are now done by using the animals for ploughing and driving the *noraj*, the threshing machine for wheat and *ful masri*. The spare labour of the tenants was then put to a different use by earning extra income from part-time activities in non-agricultural works, like brick-making, white-washing houses, digging wells, etc.

In the third phase the ideal pattern of distribution in the co-operatives is where the costs of ploughing, seeds, fertilizers and threshing are shared between the schemes and the tenant farmers. However, in some schemes there are still some claims on the tenants' production if the land is, or is assumed to be, *milk* land as the two cases in this section showed.

## Section IV Suleim[32] and Burgeig Schemes

*The Suleim Basin Scheme*

The Suleim basin is different from the land along the river banks in its organization of production land tenure, and type of crops cultivated, these being mostly cash crops for outside markets.

Production depends on small plots of ten *faddans* cultivated as independent units by small-holders. The nature of production relations is different and hence the expropriation of these peasant producers takes a different form from that of the share-cropping arrangements described earlier. The syphoning off of surpluses here, as opposed to the schemes, is indirect, and depends on the credit relations (*shayl*) existing between the peasant producers on the one side, and the traders and other financiers on the other. As I will show later (Chapter 6) the rural financiers reap their interest from marketing or financing agricultural operations and this clearly applies to the Suleim situation whereas on the schemes these capitalists are directly involved in the production process with their capital investments in land reclamation, provision of irrigation equipment, etc. In the Suleim, at least theoretically, the peasant producer 'owns' the land, the irrigation equipment and his labour, and is assumed to be independent in making decisions concerning the running of his farm. In most respects the tenancies of the Suleim basin resemble the dispersed independent *sagiyas* especially those of the Situation 'A' (see p.130). Nevertheless it is hardly possible to maintain that the Suleim peasants are totally independent producers as I will show in the analysis of the relations of production.[33]

*Land Acquisition* The Suleim scheme started as the first gravity irrigation project in the Northern Province when the *sagiya* was the main irrigation technique in the region. Being of comparatively large area (24,000 *feddans* in 1910) it was firstly planned to provide the government's food crops and fodder for troops in Egypt. The Danagla were reluctant to desert their fertile *sagiya* lands and their houses and move to the basin as the land was not that productive and needed a lot of reclamation work.[33] Moreover the basin was barren and people did not like the hot winds coming across the sandy desert and preferred to stay along the riverbank where the weather was milder. The administration then allocated most of the land to the *shaykhs* and *omdas* as well as to some Egyptian immigrants (*falaliyh*) in order to encourage the local people to take tenancies. This policy of the administration continued until the mid-twenties when the basin land had improved productivity. Those who recognized the benefits accruing to the first tenants applied for tenancies, which until then, were acquirable in any number to those who could exploit them especially when (in the 1920s) the irrigation in the basin changed gradually from the Nile flood, which means one agricultural season, to *matarat*, which allowed for more diversification of crops and continuity of work for the tenants throughout the year.[35]

This system of land acquisition by those who could exploit it contributed largely to the concentration of land holding in a small number of owners, mainly the Native Administration personnel,[36] until 1969 when the present President declared a limited land reform for the Suleim basin and the central district in general. The decisions were mainly directed to attacking the land-owners who did not actually participate in the agricultural production and appropriated most of the cultivators' surpluses. Another objective was the transformation of the Suleim basin into a controlled scheme for the production of cash crops like *ful masri*, cumin, garlic and peas which proved to grow better in the basin. A new basis for distribution was set so as to guarantee the allocation of land to those whose life depended only on cultivation. The main guidelines were:

a) land would be given to Sudanese only;[37]
b) that land should be allocated to those who actually undertook cultivation (land for the tiller was the dominant motto at that time);
c) that the plots should be of ten *feddans* (10.3 acres) as this was considered the viable unit for the maintenance of a tenant family; with special consideration for those who maintained larger families; and
d) land should not be given to those who owned land outside the basin, or tenancies in other schemes.[38]

These principles were satisfactory to the share-croppers of the Suleim, but they posed different problems, concerning allocation of tenancies, compensation of the former owners for their fixed assets, etc. Despite these problems there have been remarkable changes both in the land tenure system, as the tenants now are the legal proprietors of land, and in the relations of production.

*Relations of production* Until 1969, production relations were not different from those prevailing in the other schemes in the region (see Table IX, p.66). In most of the *matarat*, land was held by the one who owned the small pump or *sagiya*, and thus the share-cropper was entitled, as on the agricultural schemes, to half of his products in return for his labour after the deduction of the shares of the land, seeds, etc. The other half went to the owner of the pump or *sagiya* who might own the land too. The different distributions are shown on the following table (Table XI) which indicates the resemblance of this system to that in the schemes especially before 1969. Few cultivators owned their means of production (these were mostly *sagiyas* as they cost less to install than pumps), but the majority cultivated through the share-cropping arrangements typical of the schemes until 1969. In this year land was appropriated to the cultivators, but that did not resolve the problem of providing the irrigation equipment which in turn led the tenants to resort to their former landlords and traders for credit to install the necessary equipment, and to provide *shayl* for the running of their pumps and the purchase of their consumption requirements.

**Table X A Comparison between the Number of Pumps and *sagiyas* in the Suleim Basin and distribution over the different Qisms (sections) in 1969**

| | Qism 2 | | Qism 3 | | Qism 4 | | Qism 5 | | Qism 6 | | Outside Qism 2 | | Outside Qism 3 | | TOTAL | |
|---|---|---|---|---|---|---|---|---|---|---|---|---|---|---|---|---|
| | No. | % | No. | % | No. | % | No. | % | No. | % | No. | % | No. | % | No. | % |
| PUMPS | 283 | 80 | 107 | 50 | 85 | 79 | 63 | 94 | 53 | 100 | 36 | 95 | 19 | 40 | 686 | 74 |
| SAGIYAS | 71 | 20 | 107 | 50 | 22 | 21 | 4 | 6 | — | — | 4 | 5 | 29 | 60 | 237 | 26 |

Source: *Socio-Economic Survey of the Suleim Basin* by T. Abdul Mutalib, Ministry of Agriculture, Table 7, B, 1970.

As we can see from Table XI, only one-quarter of the pumps were owned by the cultivators themselves. Because of lack of statistical data after the 1969 survey of the Suleim basin, I will describe the three types of partnerships or arrangements from information I gathered in 1977.

A basic assumption following the 1969 reform is that all the land belongs to the tenants who actually undertake cultivation. Some tenants, and especially those near the towns, employ wage labour and engage in vegetable production. Others, mainly the elderly, lease their land to other share-croppers. In such a situation, keeping the ownership of the irrigation equipment apart, the share-cropper will be entitled to half of the net product after the original tenant has taken one twelfth of the total product for the land, and one half of the remainder for the pump or *sagiya*. The other half of the remainder is divided equally between the tenant and the share-cropper if the former works himself or provides a *jiygol*.

The other arrangement is where the leaseholder cannot provide the pump. Here there are different systems. In the first stages of the reform when the tenancies of the wealthy pump owners had been given to the tenants, the pump owners leased their pumps to the tenants who continued to pay half of their product after taking the share of their land, a situation not different from the previous one except in the fact that the tenants instead of the pump owners are entitled to the land rent. Agreements are concluded between some of the owners and the tenants in such a way that the tenants buy the pumps and other fixed capital items, and pay the agreed price by seasonal installments either in cash or kind in the form of agricultural products. After their agreement on the price this is solemnized by a written document and witnesses; these agreements are legally binding and in the event of default could be taken to courts.

The other way of obtaining pumps is by purchase from a trader in town. Here revolve most of the credit relationships found in the Suleim between the traders and the peasant producers. The purchase is in the form of a partnership in most of the cases investigated but the ownership of the land and the pump rests with the tenant as he is the only legal holder of the tenancy. The arrangement works as follows: the tenant takes the pump from the trader with the invoice in the name of the tenant; or otherwise the trader undertakes the payment of the price to a fellow merchant who deals in pumps and their spare parts. Then the trader and the tenant share the cost of digging the well which may be also undertaken by the trader and incorporated in their final agreement. The tenant, if he has not got ready cash will pay half of the costs in installments from his half of the produce. After the pump is installed and ready for operation, the tenant may either cultivate all his land by himself or else contract a share-cropping agreement with another *turbal*. At harvest, the distribution of the crops goes in this way; one twelfth of the crop goes to the tenant as rent for his land. Then if he is cultivating by himself, he divides the produce into two halves, one for himself and the other for the pump. Then the half for the pump is divided into two, after deducting the costs of running and maintaining the pump, which is usually paid by the trader until harvest. From his total share, the tenant, then, pays the installment for his half of the pump and installation costs. The final distribution will be as follows, distributed over the factors of production, land, capital in the form of the pump, and labour, taking the assumption of 40 *ardabs* of produce:

**Table XI* Distribution of Crops in Sukeim until 1969**

| Form | | | Land | | Pump | | Tenant | | Pump & Land | | Dulab | | |
|---|---|---|---|---|---|---|---|---|---|---|---|---|---|
| | | No.% | Share | % | Share | % | Share | % | Share | % | Share | % | Remarks* |
| 1 | 339 | 38.4 | 1/6 | 16.6 | 5/12 | 41.67 | 5/12 | 41.67 | — | — | — | — | Mostly in Qism 3 (61%) |
| 2 | 125 | 14.2 | 1/12 | 8.33 | 11/24 | 45.8 | 11/24 | 45.8 | — | | — | — | Mostly in Qism 4 (46%) |
| 3 | 74 | 8.4 | — | — | — | — | 1/2 | 50.0 | 1/2 | 50.0 | — | — | Almost all over the basin |
| 4 | 52 | 5.9 | — | — | — | — | 3/4 | 75.0 | 1/4 | 25.0 | — | — | In Qism 2 mostly (37%) |
| 5 | 226 | 25.6 | — | — | — | — | — | — | All | 100.0 | — | — | Mostly in Qism 2 and Qism 3 |
| 6 | 16 | 1.6 | — | — | — | — | | | | | | | (35% and 29% resp.) |
| 7 | 8 | 0.9 | 1/21 | 4.16 | 23/48 | 47.92 | 1/3 | 33.3 | 2/3 | 66.6 | — | — | Mostly in Qism 3 (56%) |
| 8 | 2 | 0.2 | 1/8 | 12.5 | 7/16 | 43.75 | 23/48 | 47.9 | — | — | — | — | Mainly in Qism 6 (75%) |
| 9 | 41 | 4.6 | 1/6 | 16.66 | — | — | 7/16 | 43.75 | — | — | — | — | All in Qism 4 |
| | | | | | | | 3/4 | 75.0 | — | — | 1/12 | 8.33 | These are *sagiyas*. Mostly in Qism 3 & Qism 2 (59% and 41% resp.) |
| TOTAL | 883 | 100.0 | | | | | | | | | | | |

* Arranged from Table 11(A), Abdul Mutalib, *op.cit*.

| | share in *ardabs* | % |
|---|---|---|
| Land | 3.33 | 8.33 |
| Pump | 18.33 | 45.83 |
| Tenants | 18.33 | 45.83 |

Then the tenant's share will be land rent plus half of the pump share plus half of the produce if he is cultivating himself which is equal to 30.82 *ardabs* (77 per cent of the total produce). From this he has to pay the trader's installment on his half of the pump and other costs if he is using a share-cropping *turbal*, then his initial share, 18.33 is divided between him and the share-cropper, placing the latter in the same position of the *tarabla* in the big pump schemes.

Perpetual personal ties between the traders and the tenants are important in such an arrangement, and this is why we find that such relationships have been established a long time ago, but in a different form. This personal relationship reduces the risk of non-compliance with the agreements, most of which are not obligatory in civil courts. The only form enforceable is when the agreement shows a direct partnership between the trader and the tenant in the pump like those concerning takeovers from traders by tenants and the agreed payments. The 'Agricultural Agreement' which binds the landowners and the pump owners on the riverain schemes does not function here; and to install a pump in the Suleim one should produce a tenancy registration certificate which after 1969 could only be produced by a tenant cultivator. So all the pumps should be legally registered in the name of the landholder, in this case the tenant, and here comes the importance of personal ties because in a case of a dispute over the ownership of the pump, the proof finally rests with the agricultural authorities and the name under which the particular pump is registered. So we have a situation where theoretically all the pumps in the basin are owned by the tenants whereas in fact most tenants cannot afford to buy pumps. The prospects of profits from the shares in the crops and the high interests from *shayl* relationships on the traders' side, and the difficulty in getting sufficient money to buy his own irrigation equipment on the tenants' side, work as important binding factors in concluding these agreements sanctioned by mutual trust, and dependency of the tenant producer on the financing trader on the one hand, and the customary and moral forces as to the fulfilment of debts, honouring of one's word for fear of social ridicule, etc., on the other.

*The Burgeig Government Scheme* This scheme was established in 1943/4 by the government in an area of 4,800 feddans in the northern edge of the Suleim basin (in Qism 6). It has 480 tenants on 480 tenancies. The tenants, like those of the Suleim basin, are of different tribal backgrounds, with the Danagla being the dominant group at present. This Danagla majority is comparatively recent because at the start of the scheme, the Danagla were reluctant to take tenancies as they had done in the Suleim before. So a number of tenants were brought from the neighbouring regions – Mahas, Shaigiya, Manasiyr, from the Falaliyh and the desert nomads.

*The organization of the scheme* The fact that it is a government scheme contributes to its uniqueness in the region. Unlike the private schemes along the Nile and in the basins, it has a very highly centralized organization and the tenants are almost totally under the control of the scheme management which consists of trained agricultural experts. It is run as one farm, and in many respects has to comply with the policies of the Agricultural Corporation which is a body governing all the government schemes in the country. The local policy for the scheme derives from a national policy with special consideration for the local needs of the tenants. In this is resembles the Gezira Scheme organization as far as the strategies and the organization of farm work are concerned. The only difference from the Gezira, which also constitutes a major difference (among others) from the local private schemes, is the absence of the share-cropping arrangements prevalent in both the Gezira and the local schemes Land is *miyri* and as such is allocated free for the tenants at the start of the scheme without a land rent. The cost of irrigation is paid in cash using water rates ranging from £S6 to £S20 per *feddan*, depending on the type of crop cultivated and the duration of irrigation. For seasonal crops, for example, the tenants pay £S6 for *dura* and £S8 for wheat; and for permanent crops like lucerne, date palms and fruit trees, twenty pounds are paid for a *feddan* per annum. These rates are only for the provision of water but the responsibility of the scheme does not end here as it also provides other services like extension services and crop protection. On the other hand the tenants have to provide all other requirements like seeds, fertilizers, ploughing (the first two may be supplied by the scheme for nominal prices and tractors offered for hire also) and labour for which the tenant can use his own labour or employ hired labour or share-croppers.

The water rates, added to the absence of any intermediaries[39] between the individual tenants and the administration, and the fact that the scheme is a government scheme, account for the relative strength of the tenants for collective action over the running of the scheme and the improvement of conditions of production. The unitary nature of the organization brings the tenants together in a joint interest in the scheme, in its efficient running, and the provision of irrigation and other services, and of necessary technical guidance. There was a long struggle between the tenants and the scheme as the former were seeking the right to organize themselves in a union to secure their rights.[40] These attempts precipitated a number of uprisings of a different nature uncharacteristic of the tenants in the other private schemes. In December 1976, for example, a failure in the pumps turned from being a demand for the repair of the machinery into a serious political confrontation with the provincial political authority (the Sudanese Socialist Union) and the provincial authorities. The December event, as it is referred to in the official records, started as an ordinary technical problem usually dealt with through bureaucratic and technical channels, but the failure of the administration to resolve the problem quickly drove the tenants, helped by others, to besiege the scheme buildings, to arrest the senior staff and confine them to their offices, to call for direct negotiation with the national minister concerned and to refuse to negotiate with the Provincial Commissioner and his assistants. The militancy here reflects the strength of organization, not necessarily on a union basis, in the way they developed a consciousness that promptly brought them to take joint action. This movement was peculiar to Burgeig, and it is worth asking what factors allowed such a confrontation to take place in the Burgeig and not elsewhere. For other tenants there is always the threat of the insecurity of tenure which drives them in these schemes to accept whatever is dictated or otherwise dismissed. A similar organization, or tendency like that of the Burgeig can be found in the co-operative schemes; but with the kind of problems these schemes are facing, the position of the tenants is more vulnerable if they try an action like the one at Burgeig. It is crucial that in the Burgeig tenancies, all the tenants (or their heirs) have been holding the same plots since the scheme was established in 1944. In contrast there is a high turnover of tenants in the private schemes.

I have tried in this section to show how the two schemes (Suleim and Burgeig) are different and contrast with the private schemes in the region (co-operatives, individual and company schemes). It is evident that they differ both in the relations of production and their organization, and this shows the possibilities of different consequences on the political organization of the tenants (as the Burgeig illustrates), although the tenants' political activity in the area is not yet so fully manifested in their actions as to warrant their analysis as peasants' or tenants' risings.

# Notes

1 See W. Y. Adams, *op.cit.*, p.19.

2 In 1973/4 about 21 per cent of the cultivated land was irrigated by *sagiyas* along the river banks (see Table 7, p.126). However, the *sagiyas* are mostly used for the cultivation of very small areas where a pump is not economical to run. Also there was a sharp increase in the number of *sagiyas* in 1973 when the area suffered from an acute shortage of fuel.

3 See Farah H. Adam, 'The Patterns of Agricultural Production in the Sudan', in *The Bulletin of Sudanese Studies* (in Arabic), 1972, p.32.

4 *The Suleim Basin,* a memorandum prepared by the Agricultural Inspectors' Office for the Provincial Conference on the Future of Agricultural Production in the Northern Province, Dongola, April 1976. Also al-Shahi, *op.cit.*, p.134.

5 See R. F. Wynn, *The Development, Present Economic Performance and Future Prospects of Nile Pump Irrigated Agriculture in Sudan,* University of Khartoum, 1967, Table I, p.6.

6 See Chapter One.

7 This situation has been changing, for the owners of *matarat* wells in the leasehold land and in the Suleim can plant date orchards. But on the freehold land share-cropping of dates is entirely an *ahali* concern. I will describe the earlier forms of the past since they formed the basis of wealth of many of the *ahali* group members.

8 For the composition of tenant farmers in one village, see Table III Chapter Four, p.36.

9 The excesses of the Turkish rule (1821–84) in the exaction of taxes, together with the turmoil following the rise of the Mahdi, forced many Danagla to migrate and leave their land which was appropriated by others. See *Abu Salim, al-ard fi al-Mahdiyya,* Sudan Research Unit, University of Khartoum, p.21. See also *Reports on the Province of Dongola,* Sudan Pamphlets, Vol. 15, Sudan Collection, University of Khartoum.

10 It is not yet allowed to grow permanent crops in agricultural schemes, but those who acquire rights in the *miyri* (for 99 years lease) can grow trees and they are usually wealthy individuals or partners.

11 In sandy places people used to dig a hole of two metres or so deep and then build a lining wall to prevent the sand from filling the hole and killing the shoot.

12 See T. A. Leach, 'Date-Trees in Halfa Province', in *Sudan Notes and Records,* Vol. II, No. 2, 1919, p.99.

13 Approximately one quarter of a bushel.

14 Personal communication, Mushu, May 1977.

15 It is difficult to follow all possessions in the register, except land, since the people have so many agreements which do not surface until one party to these agreements dies.

16 Seasonal crops constitute both cash crops and subsistence crops. They include wheat, *dura, ful masri,* onions, garlic, cumin, *hilba,* peas, *turmus,* chick-peas and *gurma,* the last six of which are mainly cash crops. There are also *lubiya* and clover grown mainly as fodder and for the protection of shoots. Vegetables like tomatoes, *mulukhiya,* okra, *rigla,* pumpkin, etc., are grown for consumption needs and for market, especially for the growers near the towns. The share-cropping in vegetables and fodders is basically different as the shares of schemes (or *sagiyas*) are evaluated in money.

17 See D. J. Shaw, 'The Development and Contribution of Irrigated Agriculture in the Sudan', in *Agricultural Development in the Sudan*, Vol. II, papers for the Thirteenth Annual Conference of the Philosophical Society of the Sudan, 1966, edited by D. J. Shaw, p.177.
18 See W. R. G. Bond, 'Some Curious Methods of Cultivation in Dongola Province', *Sudan Notes and Records*, Vol. VIII, 1925, p.97.
19 Compare with the price of the smallest pump and engine of Indian make which cost £S450 to buy excluding the costs of installation.
20 A *kasr* is one hundredth of a faddan (42 sq.m.)
21 *A Memorandum on the Obstacles of Agricultural Production in the Northern Province* (in Arabic), Assistant Commissioner for Agricultural Affairs, Dongola, 4th September, 1976.
22 D. J. Shaw *op.cit.*, 1966, p.178.
23 This distribution takes place after the deduction of the seeds (plus the interest if taken on loan) and the share of land which depends on the season and the crop cultivated. In the winter crops, the Nile is very low so there is much work in clearing the *kodaig*. There is also much work for the animals as the distance from the waterbase is very high. Land share is reduced to two *khushum*. In summer crops, the Nile is high and work is less for animals and the *tarabla*. Land is allowed three shares. Land rent is taken before the final distribution which follows the 'heaping' principle described for dates. The system of distribution is expressed in vulgar fractions, that is any unit is divided into twelve parts (*khushum*) so that each *khashm* equals one twelfth of the unit.
24 For detailed description see W. Nicholls, 'The Sakia in Dongola Province', *Sudan Notes and Records*, Vol. I, 1918. See also D. J. Shaw, *op.cit.*, 1966.
25 It was the custom for *sagiya* owners to leave one of their members to take care of their property in the land. Others members might migrate or be engaged in other activity and provide money for this representative (*samad sagiya*), who worked as trustee for their property, and in the case of migrants for their families also. No division usually took place for the products, especially if they were brothers, and the income from the land was taken by this one to enable him to stay and look after the property (especially date trees) and the families.
26 The sign (+) refers to the possession of the material factors and use of human labour as defined. (±) partial possession and (–) lack of possession.
27 See Chapter Four.
28 Adam argued that the control over land and irrigation equipment entitled one to 60 per cent of the product, which is true. But the way he explained it in terms of land scarcity is not convincing as land was, and is still, in abundance relative to the number of people willing to undertake cultivation. His explanation was contained in this passage: '. . . this relation reflects on the one hand the relative scarcity of land and irrigation equipment; and the relative abundance of labour power willing to participate in agricultural production despite the small proportion that accrued to it, on the other hand.' (My translation) See F. H. Adam *et al*, *On the Modernization of Agricultural Production in the Northern Region (Northern and Nile Provinces)*, Working Paper No. 24 Erkowit Annual Conference, Kareima, July 1976, University of Khartoum, p.1.
29 I came across two cases in 1977 of the persistence of the tenancy holder in two companies and one co-operative scheme. (See Case I and II in this chapter.)
30 These resolutions were later codified in the Unregistered Land Law, 1970. See the *Legislative Supplement*, *Sudan Gazette*, April 1970.
31 In 1972 the scheme rejected a proposal to change into a co-operative with the promise of more land outside the island to develop as it was financially the best of the area schemes. The secretary of the scheme told me that they rejected it for fear of strangers coming into the island.
32 This assumes the legal practice of 10 piastre/faddan rent which is obtaining in most of the schemes in the area.
33 The Suleim basin is a stretch of clay soil extending parallel to the Nile on the eastern side. It starts opposite Dongola in the south and extends to Kerma in the north. Its length is 56 kilometres and is of 5 kilometres width. The total distributed land in 1969 was 37,270 out of a total area of 51,630 *faddans*. See Abdul Mutalib, T., *Socio-economic Survey of the Suleim-Kerma Basin*, Ministry of Agriculture, Sudan, 1970.
34 In 1969, only 25 per cent (226 out of 883) of the tenants could actually claim individual ownership of the pumps. See Abdul Mutalib, *op.cit.*, Table 11A.
35 Abdul Basit Mukhtar, *A Memorandum on the Suleim Scheme*, Dongola, April 1976, p.20.
36 Although the *sagiyas* are largely replaced by pumps there were still 237 *sagiyas* at work in 1969 (26 per cent of the tenancies) see Table X.
37 A former *omda* had 82 different plots in 1969 totalling 820 feddans.

38 This was introduced as the Danagla were claiming that some of the *falaliyh* are not Sudanese, and that they, in collaboration with the Native Administration, had acquired the best of the land, etc.

39 See Abdul Basit Mukhtar, *op.cit.*, p.5.

40 Until 1954, there were *samads* to collect water rates and taxes from the tenants, but they have been abandoned, and the tenant is directly answerable to the scheme.

41 Paradoxically from 1954 to 1968 the scheme had a strong union and since then it has become weaker, to the point of non-existence.

# Chapter Six: Rural Traders and Agricultural Development

In the previous chapters the process of agricultural development was described in relation to the process of capital accumulation and investment by different elements like the government, the co-operative societies and the peasants themselves. However, the description focused on certain historical changes affecting the forces of production both in their development and in the property rights in them. Reference has already been made to the activities of different elements of the rural population especially middle or wealthy peasants and their migrant relatives who had largely influenced the changes taking place in the Danagla economy, and more directly contributed to its expansion. Another factor which has less directly influenced this development was the development of trade and the consequent integration of the local economy with the external markets which, in turn, changed the character of the traditional agricultural production and its organization from one which was characteristically subsistence to a more commercialized one. It is worth mentioning here that this influence was gradual and it affected only certain areas, Suleim basin for example; it also affected the production of certain cash crops in the beginning, a process which is not yet fully completed. The production of cash crops like broad beans *(ful masri)* garlic, cumin and peas was encouraged by the traders' search for more items of trade for the markets in Egypt and the growing internal markets, in addition to the main crop from the area in the past – dates. To establish direct links between the traders' activities and the production of these crops poses the difficulty of specifying the nature of these links as well as their magnitude. But it can be asserted here that the local economy, until the beginning of the thirties, was geared to the production of food requirements and had little exchange with the external markets. The goods exchanged were limited – dates from the area in exchange for limited items such as salt, sugar, tea etc. The change to other crops, and the extensive use of money came with the Turkish invasion of 1821, and had increased by the beginning of this century after the Anglo–Egyptian occupation of 1898. By opening external markets to the local items, and establishing and organizing internal markets, this development allowed for the easy flow of market goods and also provided an outlet for the surpluses of the local population which could be exchanged for incoming goods mainly from Egypt. Egypt also provided the personnel to carry out the trading activities in the early days of trade. Gradually local people themselves started trading and in the course of this, opened up a network of trading centres (*sugs*) in the villages which increased the range of trade within the area. The continuous demand for certain crops needed in Egypt and the national markets made the traders involve themselves progressively in the direct production of these crops instead of confining themselves to exchanging them.

This chapter addresses itself to the analysis of the role of trade and traders in the development of the rural economy by describing the history of trade; the personnel involved, and their social characteristics; and their activities which have positively influenced the progressive development of the agricultural economy of the area. The first section will be on the history of trade in which the development of market centres and communications will be described with special emphasis on the growth of rural towns as focal points for trade as well as administrative functions. The second section will be on the description of the personnel involved in trading business and related services who until the mid-thirties were mostly from Falaliyh group who dominated the external trade and the internal retailing businesses. This domination still continues in the wholesale and import/export trade of the region leaving most of the retail trade in the hands of the other Danagla groups. The demographic and social characteristics of the traders are described to show their constitution, their ethnic groups, with other characteristics. The third section will describe the different activities which provided these traders with the capital necessary to embark on agricultural investment, and the transfer of capital back and forth according to demand between trade and agriculture, or the dominant practice of investing in both simultaneously which was the dominant practice among the traders. Their inseparable activities (that is in production and financial activities as creditors) will be described as these finally enhanced their control over the peasant economy and at the same time increased their rate of accumulation and the appropriation of the peasant surpluses.

**Section I: History of Trade**

Dongola area, and the Northern Province in general, had never been important trading centres in the past, especially in the period before the Anglo-Egyptian domination after 1898. However, the area had always been important for the passage of trade between Egypt and central and western Sudan, and as the source of some of the personnel conducting this trade, i.e. merchants and retailers:

> The sedentary riverain people inhabiting the Nile reach from Khartoum to Dongola, were traditional peasants . . . These folks possessed a keen mercantile instinct and when, during the Turkish period, they were forced out of their lands by the heavy and arbitrary taxes imposed by the government, many of them abandoned agriculture and turned to trade. They dealt mainly in retail trade and distributed goods throughout the country, while some became pedlars and chapmen selling local products from village to village. However, it is doubtful whether any of these riverain people could raise enough capital for a trading journey to Egypt, the main market during this period.[1]

However during the Turkish era almost all the Sudan trade, especially that with the outside world and long distance trade, was dominated by foreigners who had enough capital to traffic their merchandise between Egypt and the Sudan. The nature of the merchandise itself made it impossible for the area to be largely affected by the trade of the time, as the goods were mostly of exotic nature like gold, ostrich feathers, gum arabic and indigo,[2] items that were, and still are, not the produce of the region. Even the influence that can be gained from the passage of trade caravans through the region was not large enough as the area did not offer a safer passage for the caravans owing to the raids of the nomads of the eastern desert. As a result the routes of trade were diverted further away from the Nile and mostly followed *darb al anba'iyn* in the western desert.[3] This, however, resulted in the isolation of the area from the external markets, and this to a large extent lessened the response of the internal market and consequently slowed the response of the local economy to the needs of the relatively developed markets in Egypt and Sudan. In the northern Sudan and in the riverain area then,

> In this early period, external trade did not stimulate internal trade which appears to have been carried on through barter entirely within the villages – the

> movement of goods between regions must have been relatively small. The reasons for this are: (a) geographical concentration of the conduct of trade; (b) inadequate and costly transport; and (c) more importantly, nearly every region could easily produce the basic items entering into the standard of living.[4]

Earlier travellers told of flourishing trade from the area in horses and emphasized the fact that the region was an important route for trading caravans between the Sudan and Egypt, but never as a source of exchanged goods or a market for imports itself. The weakening of political control along the Nile at the time of the decline of the Fung kingdom made the area unsafe as a transit route; and consequently the slight influence of trade was halted. Before then, villages such as Khandaq and Mushu were important customs stations on the trade route.[5] Nevertheless the trade as such was not important to the area as the local product did not constitute any of the trade items of that time, except dates which were outside that trade and dealt with in a different way. This resulted in the isolation of the local economy from external markets and also hampered its response to the influences of the working of market principles. The economy remained basically a subsistence one, with the production of surpluses just sufficient to furnish the individual families with what they could not produce themselves, and these they exchanged for the surpluses of other similar families in village market places. By the middle of the nineteenth century pedlars from Egypt started to bring some items that appealed to the local population, first to the local chiefs, wealthy peasants and to the ordinary people such as fine-woven cloth, tea, sugar, salt, etc. By and by the range of incoming merchandise widened and the peasants found themselves in a position to produce more surpluses to furnish the costs of these items which, since currency was scarce, could only be achieved by the direct exchange of their produce.

The intensification of the trading activities took place after 1898 when new demand was created for the products of the area, especially food crops, and trade between Sudan and Egypt was more organized. The higher demand in Egypt for the food crops, and the geographical proximity of the region, speeded up the response of the local economy to it and more land was put under cultivation to meet the increasing demand. However, this cannot be attributed to the working of the market demand in Egypt only as it was also the declared policy of the Colonial Government to increase the production of food crops. The market influence was already there especially that induced by the trade in dates; but the government not only created more demand itself by its need to feed its troops in Egypt, but also positively influenced the expansion of local production by establishing new schemes and introducing more money which made it possible for the exchange of crops and market goods to be effected by money transactions.

*Local Trade, Market Centres (sugs) and Transport* Before 1900 the regional transport, as it was throughout the Sudan, depended on animals and boats between the villages and for the little trade that existed between Egypt and the Sudan. The trading capital for the trader of the time consisted of a donkey and for big merchants it was a number of camels plus the money (or pieçes of cloth etc.) needed for the petty transactions. Until the Condominium rule money was rare and barter was the main method of exchange.[6]

With the beginning of colonial rule, effective integration of the local trade with external markets was established specially when local market centres were set up and a standard currency was introduced. Later developments were the introduction of modern river transport to connect Kerma with Kariema, the terminus of the railway line along the main Nile; the starting of a road between Dongola and Omdurman; and the introduction of telegraph and telephone services.[7] These developments made it possible for the earlier traders, who originally came from Egypt, to develop the area's trade; and having former connections with Egypt they geared the trade of the region to that of Egypt.[8]

Before settling in market centres (*sugs*) these traders used to move about in the area selling their Egyptian imports, exchanging them for the products of the area, especially dates, and natron which used to be brought down from the desert by the nomadic tribes to the markets of Dongola area. The collection of dates and its transport to Egypt led some of these traders to settle in focal points which later developed as administrative centres too. Kerma is an example of such development as a market place for the northern Danagla as well as for the southern Mahas. Argo started as an administrative centre for the ruling family of the Danagla during the Fung era, and then developed as a market centre when a large number of the Falaliyh settled there, especially after the establishment of the Burgeig Scheme in 1944. Being in the heart of a fertile island (Argo Island) and quite near to the northern parts of the Suleim and to Burgeig schemes, it developed as an important market for the agricultural products of the northern region where the population density is very high and that added to the town's importance as a centre for the distribution of market goods. Moreover, with the lack of modern transport, for example lorries, Argo was still located within easy access by boats to many of the surrounding islands and villages from both sides of the river. However, its importance has been declining as Dongola's is increasing as a result of the use of modern transport, mainly road transport and steamers' services to Kareima and from there to the other parts of the Sudan.

Dongola started as a camp for the fleeing Mamlukes in 1812 and hence its name *al ordi* (literally camp). At the end of the 19th century, it developed as headquarters for the Mahdist armies and then for the Re-Occupation Army in 1898. A number of Egyptians who were craftsmen or government employees, or returnees after the end of the Mahdists in the north, settled in the town and gradually started up crafts and trade when the local economy became geared to that of Egyptian markets and later to the national markets. So the development of the two northern markets, Kerma and Argo, can be linked to the phase when the region's trade was mainly linked with Egypt; and then they gave way to Dongola when the trade of the region became more oriented to the national markets and the development of road transport.[9]

However, the development of these three towns was the making of the colonial government which realized the need for organizing *sugs*; and also of the Falaliyh traders who started them as focal points for their hawking activities. In addition to these three towns (they are officially categorized as towns although, with the exception of Dongola, they do not possess many of the characteristics or amenities of towns) certain villages developed later as market centres for the exchange of goods, especially during the late forties and early fifties when the government set out to organize local markets. Small weekly *sugs* developed in central villages such as Hafir, Sayr, Bediyn, Amintego, Orbi and el Golid. Mainly they are places where hawkers gather, although some of them are developing permanent shops. The pattern of trade in these *sugs* still follows the old practice, started in the beginning of the century by the Falaliyh, but with a slight difference. Instead of the *tashasha* (hawkers) of the past moving about all around the area with no fixed shops, a system of gathering in these centres developed, with the traders or village traders who have shops in their permanent villages coming to them on market days to sell and also to be informed of price fluctuations of agricultural crops and other items in their vicinity.

The items of trade in these small markets are not bulky nor do they extend beyond the daily requirements of households. The merchandise is basically vegetables, meat, soap, cooking oil, beverages and some cloth, which can be easily loaded on a donkey and taken from the trader's shop to these *sugs*. However, within these *sugs* there are differences of emphasis between the established shop-keepers and those who undertake *tishasha* (petty trade) as a means of accumulating wealth so as to start a bigger business. It is usual for the bigger traders to establish permanent shops in these *sugs* which, in addition to retailing, serve as information centres and storage places. On the other hand the hawkers seem to be the biggest beneficiaries from such *sugs* as their prices are always lower than those demanded by the village shop-keepers. Moreover, the *tashasha* supply the villagers with goods in infrequent use in the households and of kinds which are very slow to sell from a village shop with a limited number of customers. The hawker then can widen the demand for such goods by moving around the *sugs* and catering for a large number of villages instead of just the one in which he normally resides.

This *tishasha* trade, according to some of the older traders who started in this way, is still the same in both the range and the scope of goods, but the personnel has changed: instead of the early Falaliyh, who originally brought this pattern of trade from Egypt, we now find that it is carried out mostly by the beginner traders, who are now nearly all from the *ahali* group. At the time when the local Danagla, specially the *ahali*, did not have many of the market goods of today, the Falaliyh started this form of trade to distribute their Egyptian imports, and consequently trade, except for very few *ahali* at the turn of the century, was the Falaliyh speciality. By and by they settled in what are now the towns of Dongola, Argo and Kerma, where they opened shops; they left the *tishasha* business to the emerging hawking class, drawn mainly from the *ahali* group, to carry the village-to-village distribution of their goods which they continued to import from Egypt and national markets in Omdurman and Port Sudan. By settling they initiated a change in the conduct of trade; instead of going to the prospective buyers in their villages and *sugs*, the buyers started to travel to these markets - a development which was accelerated by the introduction of lorries. The precedence of the Falaliyh in the trading business has precipitated important consequences on the regional trade as the other groups forming the present Danagla population were left behind in taking trade; and hence the domination, relatively in the retail business and mostly in the wholesale and import/export trade, by the Falaliyh group as Table XII shows.

**Section II: The Trading Class**

As I have shown before, the earlier traders in the area drew mainly from the migrant Egyptians (the present Falaliyh) who continued to dominate in both the wholesale and retail trade until the beginning of the forties when the *ahali*, especially those who were migrant and rich peasants, started to take over the retail trade. In this section the social and demographic characteristics of the trading class will be described as to their constitution, and occupational history, to show their development as middlemen between the peasantry and the wider markets outside, both national and international, especially that with Egypt to the north.

The material in this section is based mainly on two questionnaires conducted in the area in the period December 1976 to April 1977 among the traders. The first questionnaire is a sample survey of 10% of the retailers in the area, i.e. 86 of the registered licence-holding retailers who are just over 860.[10] The other questionnaire is a total census of wholesale licence holders (20), two of whom are sons working with fathers and also a partnership between two brothers, sharing the same capital, activities and premises which made me treat them as one wholesaler, thus making the total number 17. As most of the material presented in this work was collected from case studies, life histories, interviews with traders and other members of the Danagla community and official records, these questionnaires provide basic information of demographic and social characteristics of the traders, the scope and range of their activities and the overt participation in the social and political activities in the area.[11] They also show how these relate to the ethnic composition of the population, and indicate the consequences for other social units, e.g. the village community or the kinship groups.

At present the retail trade is mostly dominated by the *ahali* group. The Falaliyh on the other hand, although a minority, are represented by 11 out of 82 in the retail trade, that is 13.4% and 11 out of 17 in the wholesale trade, that is 64.7%. The following table (Table XII) shows the ethnic distribution of the Danagla retailers and wholesalers.

**Table XII Comparison of Ethnic Composition of the Retailers and Wholesalers**

| | Ahali | | Falaliyh | | Mahas | | Shaiqiya | | Bedayriyya | | Arabs | | Others | | Total | |
|---|---|---|---|---|---|---|---|---|---|---|---|---|---|---|---|---|
| | No. | % | No. | % | No. | % | No. | % | No. | % | No. | % | No. | % | No. | % |
| Retailers | 39 | 47.6 | 11 | 13.4 | 6 | 7.3 | 2 | 2.4 | 5 | 6.1 | 7 | 8.5 | 12 | 14.6 | 82 | 100 |
| Wholesalers | 1 | 5.9 | 1 | 64.7 | 2 | 11.8 | — | | 1 | 5.9 | — | | 2 | 11.8 | 17 | 100 |

The table above points to two important facts, viz. that the area in the past was open to incoming entrepreneurs from outside the region to start retail trade, and also that those early incomers or their children by the incidence of precedence in trade, dominate the wholesale trade in the area. The *ahali*, however, are still not represented in the wholesale trade, except for one, whereas the Falaliyh are dominant. If we add the two in the category of 'others' who are Copts, then we can see the influence that migrants of Egyptian origin have had in the area's trade. The *ahali* took trade as occupation fairly recently compared with the Falaliyh and Mahas for example. About 78% of the *ahali* retailers and the one wholesalers from that group started trading business in the last twenty years, whereas for the Falaliyh the percentages stand at 45% for both retailers and wholesalers making 55% in both forms of trade who started more than 25 years ago. The following tables (Tables XIII and XIV) show the time of starting trade for retailers and wholesalers:

So the first characteristic of the retailers is that they are mostly from the *ahali* although other groups are fairly well represented. The Falaliyh, however, used retail trade, especially *tishasha* in the past, as a step towards being settled retailers and then wholesalers – an aspiration though confessed by many yet seems unfeasible under the present conditions.[12]

The domination of non-*ahali* groups seems to have historical as well as socio-cultural causes since we find that the trader class drew from groups who had already experienced a market economy in one way or another, either as migrants outside, if from the *ahali* and the Mahas, or since they originally came from cultures where market principles had been already working as was the case in the Falaliyh. Egypt in the north has always been a source of changes in the area and its influence can be seen not only in trade, but also, as I have shown in Chapter Two, in the composition of the population; and at a later stage, the importation of certain agricultural practices and techniques especially after the introduction of basin irrigation, originally an Egyptian method. As for trade, the Falaliyh came to the area as craftsmen or soldiers with the Reconquest Army in 1898, and since then they have formed the link between the local economy and outside, especially Egypt, in trade and the transfer of different techniques in agriculture. The *ahali* at that time were mainly cultivators and considered the new crafts such as carpentry, and trade especially in wool, as inferior to agriculture. This partly explained why all these crafts were performed by foreigners to the area. Most of the traders from these foreign groups started as *tashasha* moving around in the area selling their petty goods and collecting the local products. These earlier developments set up the occupational gap between the *ahali* and others. It is difficult to assess the capacity of the local economy of the period to accommodate the ever-increasing trading activities, but what had taken place in the beginning gave the Falaliyh an advantage over the *ahali*, who when they started trade, found that it was difficult to compete with them in their trading centres of Dongola, Argo and Kerma. Most of the *ahali* traders, then, started retailing in their own villages while practising some agricultural activity; and since they lacked direct contact with external markets they had to rely on the towns' wholesalers who were, and still are, drawing from the non-*ahali* Danagla. The following table (Table XV) shows retailers and wholesalers as to their ethnic distribution and town/village orientations.

**Table XIII Distribution of Retailers by length of time, trade and tribe**

| | Ahali | | Falaliyh | | Mahas | | Shaiqiyya | | Bedayriyya | | Arabs | | Others | | Total | |
|---|---|---|---|---|---|---|---|---|---|---|---|---|---|---|---|---|
| | No. | % | No. | % | No. | % | No. | % | No. | % | No. | % | No. | % | No. | % |
| 1- 5 years | 8 | 57.1 | 3 | 21.4 | 1 | 7.1 | — | — | — | -2 | 1 | 7.1 | 1 | 7.1 | 14 | 17 |
| 6–10 ,, | 10 | 62.5 | 2 | 12.5 | — | — | 1 | 6.2 | — | — | 1 | 6.2 | 2 | 12.5 | 16 | 19.5 |
| 11–15 ,, | 3 | 33.3 | — | — | 1 | 11.1 | — | — | 1 | 11.1 | 2 | 22.2 | 2 | 22.2 | 9 | 10.9 |
| 16–20 ,, | 9 | 60 | — | — | — | — | 1 | 6.6 | 1 | 6.6 | 1 | 6.6 | 3 | 20 | 15 | 18.2 |
| 21–25 ,, | 1 | 16.6 | 2 | 33.3 | — | — | — | — | — | — | 1 | 16.6 | 2 | 33.3 | 6 | 7.3 |
| 26–30 ,, | 3 | 42.8 | — | — | — | — | — | — | 2 | 28.5 | 1 | 14.2 | 1 | 14.2 | 7 | 8.5 |
| 31- ,, | 2 | 50 | — | — | 2 | 50 | — | — | — | — | — | — | — | — | 4 | 4.8 |
| Over 35 ,, | 2 | 20 | 4 | 40 | 2 | 20 | — | — | 1 | 10 | — | — | 1 | 10 | 10 | 12.1 |

However, the present composition of the traders class is influenced to a significant by past occupation, and father's occupation. A Fallah, for example, would work as assistant to his father (5 out of 11 in the retail trade) or to a relative (2 out of 11) and then continue with the business after the principal's retirement or death; or otherwise he would start from scratch. In the beginning he would start with any craft, such as carpenter or shoemaker, from which he would collect the initial capital for trading. On the other hand most of the *ahali* traders who started trade by themselves (i.e. 25 from a total of 39) were originally cultivators, 18 out of 25 (72%), who could accumulate sufficient surpluses from agriculture to furnish them with the initial capital necessary for retailing.[13] Migration also contributed to the initial capital for the *ahali* group as we find that 15 out of 16 who had an occupation different from farming prior to embarking on trade, were working outside Dongola region (4 outside the area but in the Sudan and 11 outside the Sudan).

**Table XIV Distribution of Wholesalers by length of time in trade and tribe**

| | Ahali | | Falaliyh | | Mahas | | Shaiqiyya | | Bedayriyya | | Arabs | | Others | | Total | |
|---|---|---|---|---|---|---|---|---|---|---|---|---|---|---|---|---|
| | No. | % | No. | % | No. | % | No. | % | No. | % | No. | % | No. | % | No. | % |
| 1– 5 years | 1 | 33.3 | 2 | 66.6 | — | — | — | — | — | — | — | — | — | — | 3 | 17.6 |
| 6–10 ,, | — | — | — | — | — | — | — | — | — | — | — | — | — | — | — | — |
| 11–15 ,, | — | — | 1 | 100 | — | — | — | — | — | — | — | — | — | — | 1 | 5.8 |
| 16–20 ,, | — | — | 2 | 100 | — | — | — | — | — | — | — | — | — | — | 2 | 11.7 |
| 21–25 ,, | — | — | — | — | — | — | — | — | — | — | — | — | — | — | — | — |
| 26–30 ,, | — | — | 1 | 100 | — | — | — | — | — | — | — | — | — | — | 1 | 5.8 |
| 31–35 ,, | — | — | 2 | 50 | — | — | — | — | 1 | 25 | — | — | 1 | 25 | 4 | 23.5 |
| Over 35 ,, | — | — | 3 | 50 | 2 | 33.3 | — | — | — | — | — | — | 1 | 16.6 | 6 | 35.2 |

**Table XV Distribution of Traders (Retailers and Wholesalers) in Town/Village by ethnic belonging**

| | Retailers | | | | | | | | | Wholesalers | | | | | | | | |
|---|---|---|---|---|---|---|---|---|---|---|---|---|---|---|---|---|---|---|
| | TOWNS | | | | | VILLAGES | | TOTAL | | TOWNS | | | | | VILLAGES | | TOTAL | |
| | D | A | K | Total of Towns | % | No. | % | No. | % | D | A | K | Total of Towns | % | No. | % | No. | % |
| Ahali | — | 1 | — | 1 | 5.6 | 38 | 5.9 | 39 | 47.6 | — | — | — | — | — | 1 | 25 | 1 | 5.9 |
| Falaliyh | 4 | 5 | 1 | 10 | 55.6 | 1 | 1.5 | 11 | 13.4 | 7 | 4 | — | 11 | 84.6 | — | — | 11 | 64.7 |
| Mahas | 1 | — | — | 1 | 5.6 | 5 | 7.8 | 6 | 7.3 | — | — | 2 | 2 | 15.4 | — | — | 2 | 11.8 |
| Shaiqiyya | — | — | — | — | — | 2 | 3.1 | 2 | 2.4 | — | — | — | — | — | — | — | — | — |
| Bedayriyya | — | — | — | — | — | 5 | 7.8 | 5 | 6 | — | — | — | — | — | 1 | 25 | 1 | 5.9 |
| Arabs | 1 | — | — | 1 | 5.6 | 6 | 9.4 | 7 | 8.5 | — | — | — | — | — | — | — | — | — |
| Others | 3 | 1 | 1 | 5 | 27.7 | 7 | 10.9 | 12 | 14.6 | — | — | — | — | — | 2 | 50 | 2 | 11.8 |
| Total | 9 | 7 | 2 | 18 | 100% | 64 | 100% | 82 | 100% | 7 | 4 | 2 | 13 | 100% | 4 | 100% | 17 | 100% |
| % | | | | 22% | | 78% | | | | | | | 67.5% | | 23.5% | | | |

D, A and K stand for the towns of Dongola, Argo and Kerma.

So a pattern which existed in the mid-thirties of the previous occupation still works although the personnel might be changing. Purves writing in 1935 noted that

> After agriculture, the chief occupation of the inhabitants is petty trade. The aim of every servant and of every artisan seems to be to save enough capital to open a small shop and the number of petty traders is in excess of the requirements of the population.[14]

In contrast we find that nearly half of the Falaliyh inherited or continued with the father's trading occupation. The following table (Table XVI) compares the different groups of the Danagla as to the father's occupations which at the same time points to the fact that family ties are of importance in the running of the Falaliyh businesses.

The figures above tend to show that those who came originally from outside the area, particularly the Falaliyh, and the category of Others which includes some Copts, have a higher percentage of trading tradition than the rest. At the same time cultivation, which at the productive age of the fathers depended mainly on the ownership of the *milk* land to which the non-*ahali* could hardly have access was the predominant occupation of the *ahali*, the Bedayriyya and the Mahas as well.[15] 67% of the *ahali*, 60% of the Bedayriyya, 50% of the Mahas are from a farming background, compared with 27% of the Falaliyh and 25% of the Arabs in the retail trade. The percentages are almost reversed when we look into those whose fathers were traders as 75% of the Others, 45% of the Falaliyh, 20% of the Bedayriyya, 16% of the Mahas, 10% of the *ahali* and none in the Arab category had their fathers as traders in the retail trade. When we compare these figures with the wholesale trade there seems to be no great difference. Most of the present wholesalers (12 out of 17, that is 70%) had their fathers as traders - all the *ahali*, the Mahas, the Bedayriyya, three quarters of the Falaliyh and half of the Others. The Falaliyh here show a different pattern. Although trade was the dominant occupation of the fathers (73%), yet one was a farmer, one a labourer and two had other occupations; this points to the primacy of taking retail trade to establish themselves, and then later to expand business to become wholesalers.

In the foregoing pages I intended to describe the trading class in brief showing their composition as one class of entrepreneurs different from the rest of the population. Despite their ethnic variety, and the scope and range of their trading activities, yet they shape one basic characteristic which attracted my attention: they contributed directly or indirectly to agricultural development either through direct investment or by contributing to the finance and credit facilities for agriculture. However, their involvement has been different at the different stages of development.

In the following section, I will try to describe their activities in trade and agriculture, concentrating mainly on the latter, by looking into their direct agricultural investments and their financial and credit roles.

## Section III: Agricultural Credit and Investment

In this section the activities of the traders are described especially those pertaining to their investment in agriculture and their role as providers of credit for agricultural operations. Some reference has been made to their activities before, especially those which have direct impact on the expansion of production.

The accumulation of wealth for these traders can be described by looking into three of their main activities in the area, namely trade, direct agricultural investment and *shayl*. Brief mention will be made of their auxilliary services such as lorries, boats, flour mills, bakeries, etc. which contribute, especially now, to the intensification of their activities to embrace most of the Danagla economic activities. A number of them are extending their investments in the building and services industries in other big towns of the Sudan.[16]

**Table XVI Distribution of Traders (Retailers and Wholesalers) by Ethnic Group and Father's Occupation**

| | Retailers | | | | | | |
|---|---|---|---|---|---|---|---|
| | Trader | Farmer | Govt. Official | Labourer | Other Occupa-tions | No. Work | Total |
| Danagla | 4 | 26 | 1 | 5 | 3 | — | 39 |
| % | 10.2% | 66.6% | 2.5% | 12.8% | 7.6% | -- | 100% |
| Mahas | 1 | 3 | — | 1 | 1 | — | 6 |
| % | 16.6% | 50% | | 16.6% | 16.6% | | 100% |
| Shaiqiyya | 1 | — | — | — | — | 1 | 2 |
| % | 50% | | | | | 50% | 100% |
| Bedayriyya | 1 | 3 | — | 1 | — | — | 5 |
| % | 20% | 60% | | 20% | | | 100% |
| Arabs | — | 4 | — | 1 | 2 | — | 7 |
| % | | 57% | | 14.3% | 28.6% | — | 100% |
| Falaliyh | 5 | 3 | — | 1 | 2 | — | 11 |
| % | 45.4% | 27.2% | | 9% | 18.1% | | 100% |
| Others | 9 | 3 | — | — | — | — | 12 |
| | 75% | 25% | | | | | 100% |
| Total | 21 | 42 | 1 | 9 | 8 | 1 | 82 |
| | 25.6% | 51.2% | 1.2% | 10.9% | 9.7% | 1.2% | 100% |

Percentages are from the respective ethnic groups

Wholesalers

| Trader | Farmer | Govt. Official | Labourer | Other Occupations | No. Work | Total |
|---|---|---|---|---|---|---|
| 1 | — | — | — | — | — | 1 |
| 100% | — | | | | | 100% |
| 2 | — | — | — | — | — | 2 |
| 100% | | | | | | 100% |
| — | — | — | — | — | — | — |
| 1 | — | — | — | — | — | 1 |
| 100% | | | | | | 100% |
| — | — | — | — | — | — | — |
| 7 | 1 | — | 1 | 2 | — | 11 |
| 73.6% | 9% | | 9% | 2 | | 100% |
| 1 | — | — | 1 | — | — | 2 |
| 50% | | | 50% | | | 100% |
| 12 | 1 | — | 2 | 2 | — | 17 |
| 70% | 5.8% | — | 11.7% | 11.7% | | 100% |

The description of the trading activity, although very important as the basis of their accumulation of wealth, is not described in detail here. It is assumed that it can be understood from the description of the *shayl* system. This works in two ways, as a means of expropriating more surpluses from the peasants and also as a means of exchange of goods – distribution of the incoming market goods and the siphoning off of agricultural products from the region to the national and international markets, an activity in which the village shop-keepers and the town merchants participate in different ways. Profits from these exchanges, along with those from the *shayl* relations, furnished them with the necessary capital for initial investment in agriculture and in the expansion of their economic activities in trade and other services.

A. The *shayl*[17] System:

A general characteristic of the *shayl* is the advancement of loans (in cash or kind) against redemption from standing crops – a practice which is widespread in central and western Sudan – and usually concluded between the small village shop-keeper and the cultivators. The relationship is used as a means of syphoning peasants' surplus in two ways: in production through the system of share-cropping and in finance by providing high-interest credits. Interest on the *shayl* was estimated by some writers to be as high as 200% in the Sudan in general.[18] But in the absence of formal credit institutions the high interest rate does not stop the peasant farmers from seeking credits from private individuals, and in this case the village shop-keeper is the accessible source. From a survey conducted in 1963/64 it was found that 81% of those obtaining credits got them from private individuals.[19] So agricultural credit (in its different forms) could be obtained by peasants either from relatively wealthy villagers or else from traders.

There are, however, different types of credit relationships. On the one hand there is the relationship involving the shop-keeper and the peasants as well as other members of the community; and on the other hand there is the one involving the town merchant and the village shop-keeper, which is mostly a formal relationship decided by the working of market principles. Other credit relations do exist between crop merchants as financiers and the big agricultural schemes: the scheme would have an account with the merchant who would finance the purchase of spare parts, fuel, etc., and expect the redemption of his credits in crops. In any case the traditional definition of the *shayl*, *rammiya*, will not apply to the working of the shop-keeper – big merchant relationship, nor to that of the latter with the big agricultural producers in the area.

*rammiya:* In this traditional form of credit, the shop-keeper advances loans, mostly in the form of consumer goods and, in a few cases, cash in the pre-harvest-period, against redemption from the future crops. Formerly, especially under the *sagiya* system, transactions in kind were the only practical forms of exchange since cash was not readily available either to the lender or the borrower. So the arrangement was to agree on a price for the future crop, and such a price was invariably set well below the anticipated market price in the new season. At the harvest time, the peasant would supply the shop-keeper with an amount of grain or dates at the agreed price to cover his debts. Sometimes the peasant might run short of grain supply in the pre-harvest time when the prices are relatively high. So the debt would be registered in terms of money. At harvest the borrower should supply the equivalent of the debt in grain or dates calculated at the post-harvest prices. The system can be illustrated by this simple example: the peasant takes his household needs and his seeds from the shop-keeper with the option of repaying in cash or kind at any time. But usually the lender advances the loan with a keen interest in the benefits accruing from redemption in kind, that is grain. This will allow him a dual profit from the difference between the pre-fixed price and the current buying price, which constitutes his interest in the loan as well as profits from marketing his original consumer goods, and from selling the grain to outside markets or the non-cultivators of the village. However, the rate of interest here cannot be easily established as the agreements are usually dyadic, and although widely practised, yet kept as a personal relationship between the individual peasant and the money lender. Mutual trust and the need of the peasant together work to sustain such a practice.[20] A peasant might take a sack of wheat at the price of £S9 in the pre-harvest period. At harvest he would not only repay the sack but had also to provide grain equivalent in value to the first sack at the current price of wheat. By this time the price of a sack might fall to £S6 and the farmer, therefore, had to give 1½ sacks for the redemption of his debt.

*garoora:* The other arrangement which depends on price fluctuation but which is more profitable to the lender is to fix a price for the future crops. This differs from *rammiya* in that it has no limit to the borrower's debts, but the price of his dates, wheat, garlic, etc., depending on the next harvest, are pre-fixed. They may agree on say £S5 for a sack of wheat in the post harvest period, and then the peasant would start taking his household needs which may amount to the value of, say £S15. At harvest the peasant has to provide three sacks of wheat. So if the post-harvest price was £S6, then the shop-keeper is making £S3 interest on the credit advanced on his goods (consumer) as well as the original profits he is entitled to in the process of retailing.

In both *rammiya* and *garoora* there is the element of time and, more importantly, the facilities of storage and transport to crop markets available to the shop-keeper. In the past, storage was important as it allowed the shop-keeper to collect the crops, and then with a large quantity he could afford to hire a sailing boat to take the crops to the markets, especially those of Wadi Halfa and Egypt when dates were almost the only cash crop from the area. Transport was important as well and at present the wide use of lorries has given advantages to both peasant and shop-keeper. The peasant now had the choice of selling his crops to the village trader or taking them to the town markets, a decision which he would evaluate in terms of the benefits gained from the differences of the village's and town's price. Quantity here is decisive; the more the peasant has, the more likely he is to take his crops to the town himself, especially if he is thinking of a major shopping trip. However, I can see the development of transport and the spread of markets near to the peasants' dwellings have worked to change the character of *garoora* and to almost abolish *rammiya* in most of the villages. With the relative abundance of cash from remittances or part-time casual work, the peasant is capable of practising *garoora* in a different form. Like other salaried people he can have a book account which would be settled in cash without any obligation on his crops.

*Retailer-wholesaler credit relations:* Some of the village traders would not be able to practise *rammiya* or *garoora* with their limited resources, or provide storage for the grains collected. Also to involve himself in such relationships a trader would need ready cash to supply his debtors, the villagers, and to underwrite the purchase of his shop merchandise. In the absence of sufficient cash, the small shop-keeper will have to contract himself to a bigger trader, usually a town wholesaler and crop merchant combined, to supply him with the consumer goods which are sold to the peasants on a *shayl* basis. After the primary redemptions at the village level between the retailers and his customers, the post-harvest period is the redemption time of secondary debts between the village retailer and the big merchant.

The relationship between these traders is more organized and is free of the sort of profiteering the small shop-keeper would wring from the peasant. The bond here is that of mutual interest in securing profitability at different levels. The big merchant who is mainly an importer of consumer goods into the area and an exporter of agricultural products from the area, will maintain his relationship with any possible number of village traders as long as that would ensure a constant flow of his merchandise to his stores in the form of incoming agricultural crops and the out-going consumer goods. Similarly, the small trader would maintain such a relationship as long as it ensured a continuous flow of consumer goods on interest free credit from the merchant as well as securing a permanent outlet for his collected crops.[21] Furthermore, these crops will underwrite the price of consumer goods purchased by the wholesaler from the national markets in Omdurman, Port Sudan and formerly Egypt. The profits of these merchants then, are not totally realized in the local markets, nor are they separable from those of their trading activities in the national markets where bigger specialized institutions take the process further.

B Direct Investment in Agriculture:

As I have shown earlier, agricultural investment in the region depends largely on the availability of capital to provide irrigational equipment for what were once relatively unlimited areas of cultivable land. The traders, then, started by installing *sagiyas* to exploit the accessible *miyri* land near the river course or by digging *matarat*, wells. This was intensified by the introduction of diesel-driven pumps which started in the mid-thirties. At that time the level of individual accumulation was not enough to furnish the costs of individual private pumps, except for a very few people (mainly foreigners) whose wealth mainly originated from outside the region. By 1916, Mina, a Coptic merchant in Dongola, and Joseph Rashid, a Coptic medical assistant with the invading army, were the first to start pump schemes in the region near the town of Dongola, and these were mainly for the production of vegetables and fruits to meet the town's demand. Shortly after the leader of a religious sect, *Idriysiyya*, based in Southern Egypt, started a big scheme north of Dongola which was eventually bought by one of the Falaliyh merchants of Argo. So it is difficult to maintain that the local traders were the first to start agricultural investment in the area as they were mainly interested in conducting their petty trade at that stage of the region's development. Precedence in investment for the local Danagla can be attributed mostly to the middle peasants and petty traders, who, under the *sagiya* system were able to invest more in the *sagiya* or animals, like the case of the *samad moiya*, or otherwise through the remittances sent from outside by emigrant relatives which were invested in *sagiyas* or in the co-operative companies of the thirties. The active role of the traders followed the initiative of the emigrants in establishing these 'co-operatives'. For the traders the partnerships and co-operatives were favourable. The loss of the pump and other equipments would be too big for one or two of the emerging traders to take the full risk. However, by controlling the co-operatives they could ensure some profits from marketing their products and if the scheme was successful, high dividends on their shares. Being the only local residents who could afford any considerable amount of cash, they did not hesitate to take shares in these ventures; and being relatively the most informed from among the villagers they were able to take the responsibilities of administering the schemes on behalf of other share-holders. So in the beginning, from the mid-thirties until the mid-forties, there dominated this pattern of traders' involvement in agriculture, which differs from the one that followed after the mid-forties. The latter trend was towards individual and partnership investment in big schemes with larger areas of land. This followed the late thirties boom for food crops. Big traders, who were running businesses outside but who were originally from the area, started their own individual schemes or in partnership with resident entrepreneurs in the area. The rush of these traders was summed up by Hewison in 1948:

> The high war-time prices of food crops have attracted many of the merchant classes to agriculture, in the belief that they can and with no previous experience amass fortune from land . . . neither has any real interest in farming, and neither is prepared to do anything more than exploit the soil and the peasant farmers.[22]

This tendency cropped up towards the end of the forties to produce two of the then biggest schemes in the region – Akkad Scheme started by Osman Salih, a famous export/import merchant in Port Sudan, and Mirghani el Sayiyd in el Golid who was a merchant in Western Sudan. Both started these schemes in their villages of origin, and their schemes are still very successful especially that of Mirghani el Sayiyd (Gana'a Agricultural Company). Afterwards and following the 1948 Co-operatives Ordinance which largely influenced the investments in the early fifties, the area saw an expansion of co-operative schemes and a decline in the establishing of big individual schemes. By 1956 a different development ensued in the area, which was a remarkable shift towards the increase of small individual pumps, either on the *sagiya* land or on *matarat* which most traders used for the production of vegetables, fruits, cash crops beside small parts under stable crops. From the questionnaires conducted in 1977 certain characteristics emerged from the study of those traders who had pumps, the tables for which are listed on the following page.

**Table XVII Classification of pumps by size**

| Size of pump | Retailer's pumps | | Wholesaler's pumps | |
|---|---|---|---|---|
| | No. | % | No. | % |
| 1″ to 5″ | 24 | 80 | 2 | 28.5 |
| 6″ to 12″ | 4 | 13 | 4 | 57.2 |
| 13″ to 24″ | 2 | 7 | 1 | 14.3 |

**TABLE XVIII Classification by age of pump**

| Age | Retailer's pumps | | Wholesaler's pumps | |
|---|---|---|---|---|
| | No. | % | No. | % |
| Less than 5 years | 9 | 30 | 2 | 28.5 |
| 6–10 years | 12 | 40 | 3 | 42.8 |
| 11–15 years | 5 | 17 | 1 | 14.3 |
| 16–20 years | 3 | 10 | 1 | 14.3 |
| 21–25 years | 1 | 3 | — | — |

**TABLE XIX Classification by number of pumps owned**

| No. of pumps | Retailer's pumps | | Wholesaler's pumps | |
|---|---|---|---|---|
| | No. | % | No. | % |
| One | 22 | 73 | 2 | 28.5 |
| Two | 3 | 10 | 2 | 28.5 |
| Three | 5 | 17 | 3 | 43 |

In the first sample of small traders, 30 (37%) own pumps with different sucking capacity, but they are mostly dominated by small sucking pipe calibre (1″ to 5″) which could irrigate up to 25 faddans, and these form 80% of the small traders' pumps. Another characteristic of these pumps is that most of them (87%) are fairly newly installed in the last fifteen years. Compared to those owned by wholesalers the pattern seems to be the same, but the difference is in the sizes and areas cultivated. Only 18% (compared to 80% in the retailers' pumps) are in the category of 1″ to 5″ calibre). The category 6″ to 12″ represents 57% of the wholesalers' pumps (compared to 13% in the retailers'). Moreover most of the small traders (22 out of 30, that is 73%) have only one pump and those who have two or more represent 27%. For the wholesalers those with one represent 28%, whereas those with two or more stand for 72% of the pump owners. In this category of more than one the Falaliyh, of the town of Dongola, alone represented 57% of the owners which is because of the special relationship between some of the big merchants in Dongola and the tenants of the Suleim basin.[23]

The foregoing description suggests two points: firstly, that the wholesalers were originally retailers who could accumulate the necessary capital to invest in agriculture by buying such pumps, and secondly, the sizes of their pumps point to the chances of annexing either unregistered *miyri* land or incorporating the holdings of others, which was possible before the mid-sixties, hence the comparatively big sizes of their holdings. On the other hand the retailers' pumps, in addition to their being small in size, also show the tendency for more fragmentation, hence small amounts of land are cultivated and numerous small pumps are not economical to run and maintain.

It has been reported that for the Northern Province (including the present Nile Province), in the period between 1957 and 1972 the number of small pumps had increased to form 90% of the working pumps whereas they formed only 70% of the total number in 1957.[24] In Dongola District this holds true if we look into the number of pumps and sizes of land under cultivation in a comparable period (1957-1969). It is found that the average size of land per pump was falling fivefold showing the trend that despite the increase in numbers, the actual cultivated land did not increase proportionally, and also pointing to a process of disintegration whereby the land of a would-be big scheme, or an existing one, was distributed among a greater number of small pumps (See Table XX).

**TABLE XX Changes in Numbers of pumps and land cultivated between 1955 and 1969**

| Year | No. of pumps | Area cultivated in Faddans | Average area/pump |
|---|---|---|---|
| 1955/56* | 57 | 20,545 | 360 |
| 1964/65 | 279 | 32,300 | 115 |
| 1965/66 | 305 | 31,960 | 104 |
| 1966/67 | 329 | 32,932 | 100 |
| 1967/68 | 377 | 34,988 | 92 |
| 1968/69 | 406 | 29,067 | 71 |

* Source: Figures for 1955/56 are taken from H. M. A. Sharfi's *A Directory to Merowe – Dongola District*, Khartoum, 1957, p.47. Other figures are compiled from the years' respective *Annual Reports*, Assistant Commissioner for Agricultural Affairs Office, Dongola.

The process of disintegration, especially that initiated by town traders for vegetable and fruit production has started what can be described as capitalist farming. Although in its embryonic stage, as the traders started to transfer part of their profits accumulated from trade to the agricultural production under the different share-cropping arrangements, described in Chapter 5, or using wage labour as is the case for the town traders who run vegetable gardens and fruit orchards.

## Notes

1 See Hassan Abdul Aziz Ahmed, 'Some factors hampering the Development of Sudanese Trade During the 19th Century.' *Sudan Journal of Economic and Social Studies*, Volume II, No. 1, Summer 1977, p.32.

2 See Beshai, Adel Amin, *Export-performance and Economic Development in Sudan 1900–1967*, Ithaca Press, London 1976, p.21.
3 Hassan Abdul Aziz Ahmed, *op.cit.*, p.33.
4 Beshai, Adel Amin, *op.cit.*, p.23.
5 For a long time Mushu had been a customs station on the north frontiers of the Fung kingdom. The kings of Argo had full control over the flow of trade between Sudan and Egypt on behalf of the Fung.
6 In fact until now a form of barter is practised whereby small measures of dates or grain can be taken by a shop-keeper for items of small value, like a small weight of salt.
7 All these services were started in order to further the pacification of the country, or, like the Kerma railway line, as a military requirement.
8 Halfa traders, who were either Falaliyh or Egyptians acted as intermediaries between the Danagla and the Egyptians.
9 It has been observed that a number of Argo traders have moved to Omdurman in the last ten years, but they still maintain contacts with relatives who are traders in Argo, either as suppliers of market goods or as distributors of cash crops from the area. This is considered as an indicator of the decline of Argo town as a trading centre.
10 Three of these I could not find at the time of the survey and one was dropped in the analysis for technical error, making the sample of *82* on which the analysis is based.
12 The prospects of being wholesalers are declining now for retailers as the present big wholesalers are already dominating the business and expanding at such a rate that it is difficult for the aspirant to catch up with them.
13 The share-cropping arrangements described under the *sagiya* and small pumps provided those who were relatively wealthy with such surpluses.
14 W. D. C. L. Purves, 'Some Aspects of the Northern Province', in J. A. de C. Hamilton, (editor), *The Anglo-Egyptian Sudan from within*, London, 1935, p.175.
15 Mahas are cultivators in their homeland, so we find a similar pattern to that of the *ahali* prior to their movement from the homeland.
16 A merchant from the Falaliyh of Argo who is also a big farmer is building a residential and office block in the centre of Khartoum; and another Fallah from Dongola is building similarly. Also there are a number of small hotels in Khartoum which are owned by some of the *ahali* traders in partnership with some of their migrant villagers who had gained experiences and money from Saudi Arabia and the Gulf States enabling them to run such businesses.
17 *shayl* is a system of credit, the payment of which necessitates the mortgage of crops in advance before the harvest to the lender. This form of *shayl* is referred to locally as *rammiya.* This earlier form, however, has been declining – it has assumed another character as well as other forms. Remittances from migrant relatives, the development of modern transport and the relative availability of ready cash have largely lessened the dependence on this system of credit for the peasant and tenant farmers alike.
18 See D. J. Shaw, 'The Effects of Money-lending (Sheil) on Agricultural Development in the Sudan' in D. J. Shaw (ed.) *op.cit.* Also see M. W. Wilmington, 'Aspects of Money-lending in Northern Sudan' in *The Middle East Journal*, 1955, pp.139–146.
19 See *Report on the Sample Census of Agriculture for the Year 1964/65 in the Northern Provinces of the Sudan*, Department of Statistics, Khartoum 1969, p.58.
20 A tenant in Akkad also runs a shop from which his fellow tenants take their needs. For him, in his own words, his relationship to them is that of *garoora* only, but his 'friends' can offer him other services. On the side of his 'friends' they alleged that he practices *rammiya* like the others, but it is easier for them to deal with him in deferring debts etc. than with the others.
21 However, there is a form of *rammiya* between specialized crop merchants and some village shop-keepers which is different from that between the retailer and peasant. More likely the retailer would work as an agent rather than an independent crop purchaser from the peasant, and for that he receives a commission (10 piastres per collected sack). This works only for dates in the two cases I came across in the area, Binna Island and Hafir.
22 See J. W. Hewison, 'Northern Province Agriculture' in Tothill (ed.) *op.cit.*, p.755.
23 For that special relation see Chapter 5.
24 See Farah H. Adam, 'Patterns of Agricultural Production in the Sudan', in *The Bulletin of Sudanese Studies*, Vol. 4, No. 1, 1972, p.32.

# Conclusion

I have attempted to study the process of social change in the Danagla community resulting from the agricultural developments which took place during the last eighty years or so. Change is presented here as a dominant shift from an economy based on independent households which constituted units of production as well as units of consumption to one which is more and more characterized by increasing individualization where the individual tenant is becoming the focus of economic activity in place of the extended family under the *sagiya* system. The processes involved in such a transformation are believed to rest in the forces and conditions of production, hence this study mainly deals with the different limitations and constraints affecting the development of these factors. A major concern is the causes determining the transformation of certain elements, while at the same time being themselves influenced by other factors of which some originate in the local socio-economic structure and others outside. The changes in kinship organization and its functions, and in the division of labour, are consequences of changes affecting the rate of expansion of agricultural production. This in turn is affected by the working of factors partially located outside agricultural production-trade, migration, government policies, etc. In describing these changes the factors have been analysed to show their causal relationships, and their influence on the Danagla kinship and economic organizations. Under the *sagiya* (Situation A) the two were interrelated and inseparable, as the relations of production then were constituted in the kinship relations; and also the base of economic activity was limited both socially and physically – by the fact that the land (*milk*) was limited, and the ownership of it, and of the means of irrigation was restricted to the kinship group which worked on it. So change is presented in this book as a dominant shift from kinship relations of production as symbolized in the *sagiya* system to more or less commercialized and secular relations of production; that is change from self-sufficient production/consumption units which provided their labour requirements, to wage-labourers in the orchards and farms of the present-day rural capitalists.

The changes experienced were induced by the restructuring of the means of production and changing property relations in them which followed technical developments which revolutionized production by introducing new irrigational equipment that extended the areas under cultivation. These developments have been described in Chapters Four and Five, which aimed to show the relationship between the different forces and how they were influenced from within the area and outside; and also the consequences of these influences on the property relations and the systems of distribution of products. (Chapter 5).

To understand the sources of these developments, an analysis of the process of wealth accumulation both in agriculture (Chapter 5) and trade (Chapter 6) was then made. From the analysis presented in these chapters it has been shown how the local factors (that of capital accumulation and investment in general) can play an important role in transforming the peasant economies without, however, direct intervention from outside the economy. This does not mean that the book described a situation totally autonomous and separated from the working of industrial western capitalism. On the contrary it has established the indirect link between the Danagla economy and international capitalism through the analysis of the working of trade, i.e. at the exchange level. Nevertheless the organization of production is still, and would be for a long-time to come, based on the pre-capitalist mode of production dominant in the Danagla economy. This gave rise to the necessity for the analysis of the nature of merchant capital, its accumulation, and its expansion through trading activities and agricultural investment. A contrasting situation was briefly mentioned in the introduction, that of the Gezira scheme where capital accumulation and regeneration, at least at the time of its inception, took root outside and was an extension for the activities of industrial capital in England. In Dongola, however, it was not the articulation between industrial capitalism and the local economy that created what can be called partially capitalist and partially pre-capitalist relations of production. It was the working of local capital in the peasant economy that determined its own logic of development by adjusting itself to new demands of the local peasant markets, or those imposed later by inter-regional and international exchange. The latter has definitely influenced production, as I have shown, but not to the extent of claiming that the semi-capitalist developments here are necessarily derived from western capitalism and its organization. Petty trade in Dongola was the only means of accumulating wealth in money apart from migration (which started later than trade). The economic and social qualifications of these traders allowed them to influence some changes in agricultural production under the existing technical conditions – installation of *sagiyas* and *matarat* for share-cropping. However, the origin of wealth for these traders was in the heart of the agricultural production, except for the earlier pedlars who came from Egypt. Even for these the intensity of their trading activity was functionally related to other non-agricultural productive activities as they were also involved, besides trade, in different crafts like carpentry, blacksmithing, shoe-making etc.

With the increasing activities of traders, migrants and those in the government concerned with agricultural production, the *sagiya* was not a suitable technique for coping with the increasing demands on the peasant surpluses. The limitations on production set by the *sagiya* (Chapter 4) necessitated changes that started from the technical requirements of production. Alternative means of irrigation were introduced which required relatively large amounts of money and other resources that the peasants were not able to meet. The surpluses and savings under *sagiya* production (especially under situation A)[1] were very limited. The savings of individual units which could be concentrated only in the hands of the head of the *sagiya* provided limited investments – repair of the machine, the addition of a small plot of land, which depended wholly on the ability to purchase extra animals, etc. With the development of share-cropping in the *sagiya* system of production then, we can see when expansion took place. Here real relations of exploitation started when the peasant could solicit the surplus labour of his fellow peasants or of the settling nomads and the Sudaniyya. Exploitation did exist with the *sagiya* but it was limited to the family members and as such did not influence the social relations of peasants within one locality in the way that exploitation developed from share-cropping did. With this last development, the level of co-operation in production shifted a step further from the kinship group by incorporating others – an important step in the removal of kinship relations from being the relations of production (situation C). The household would use share-croppers (*tarabla*) when it had saved sufficient surpluses to invest in more animals to cultivate their unused *milk* land and further annex more *miyri* through the right of frontage by installing an extra *sagiya*. Otherwise, and to hasten the process of saving and accumulation, a member of the household would migrate, and remittances he sent back would furnish the necessary savings to install *sagiyas*, annex more land or plant date trees. The process of capital accumulation then became more complex and the different savings activities became more inseparable as well. This required analysis on more general lines since quantitative data was not easy to collect.

However, the ability to diversify and expand production as a whole was limited by techno-environmental factors e.g. lack of rains and the necessity of mechanical irrigation in the region; but for the individual *sagiyas* these limitations could be overcome by increased savings and investment which in turn were constrained by the availability of sufficient cash and other resources, labour power for example. The process of accumulation of wealth and its investment was incidental to the *sagiya* system of production, as the system was totally geared to the production of subsistence crops and a little surplus to meet the value of market goods. This, even after the use of share-cropping, generated limited surpluses the production of which has precipitated slight changes on the forces of production, especially land and its ownership, but these were not radical.

The radical changes came from sources external to peasant production, yet locally based, and these generated a different pattern of development in the peasant economy. Merchant capital penetrated agriculture with the intention of producing cash crops for outside markets. As I have shown in Chapter 5, the intrusion of earlier trade had created the social conditions necessary for expanded production, yet the technical conditions were not suitable for that expansion. The installation of more *sagiyas*, and small pumps and other activities, would not satisfy the traders' drive for more profits. On the other hand there were ever-increasing claims on the peasants and tenant cultivators so as to meet the requirements of market goods and other claims like government taxes, and ceremonials which tended to incorporate new and costly items of consumption. The conditions were then favourable to the activities of these traders and the peasant cultivators alike. The introduction of the 'Co-operative Companies' and other joint ventures was profitable to the traders and constituted a smaller risk for their capital (see p.79). The benefits for the peasants were obvious as they had absolute increases in their shares with less input of labour. This is what the rural capitalist realized a long time ago and he consequently retained the system of distribution of the *sagiya* despite the changes in the forces of production and the property rights in them. It is contrary to a theoretical position held by Marx which states that whenever the forces of production experience considerable changes, then the relations of production would follow suit.[2] They did follow as the course of development reflects here, but they underwent minor changes reflected in the distributional system. The *ahali* for example still have the major control of the means of production although others have equal chances to own land and pumps. There seemed to be a change in personnel and the character of the control which is important for the analysis of development in this area. However, no quantitative data could be produced to calculate the rate of exploitation of the peasants but the available data which are calculated from distributional principles suggest a steady proportional distribution in absolute terms with the difference in the schemes (Phase 1, see p.56). However that phase represented the highest exploitation rate for the *tarabla*, although their share was at the same percentage under *sagiya* share-cropping. The *turbal* under the *sagiya* provided both his labour and some of the capital assets of production and for that he was able to share up to 60% of his produce, but after the introduction of the capital intensive methods he could hardly contribute to the capital assets except marginally in the form of meagre shares in co-operatives.

A major question then arises: why has the *sagiya* system of production, with its various manifestations, survived despite the changes in the forces and conditions of production? The emerging productive capital has not changed the system of distribution, or the organization of agricultural work. The share-cropping of the two variants under the *sagiya* (C and D) still exists depending on the nature of the rights in the means of production. Apart from the changes in the means of production (right in land and pumps) the *sagiya* system has experienced slight changes. The kinship relations no longer determine the rights in land and the capital equipment has been alienated from the kinship group (except in small pumps described for the Suleim and a few along the river bank). In the schemes the kinship groups no longer regulate the transfer of property or own the capital assets; and the kinship relations are no longer the relations of production. The main productive land has been secularized and is considered as an inseparable part of the same enterprise, the scheme with its pumps and land. The tenants in the schemes are free to move from one plot of land to another and also from one scheme to another depending on one's choice and the opportunities opened in the new scheme. All these can be done irrespective of any constraints set by kinship or community ties as long as the new scheme is within the vicinity of the tenant's residence.

The kinship ties are still working, but their functions have changed and are now confined to activities far removed from the process of agricultural production[3] except for the tenants' immediate family of wife and children to help with some tasks in the field (see p.28).

The situation described in the Suleim basin and Burgeig governmental scheme depicts a different development, yet regarding labour resources and organization of work is not different from that dominant in the schemes along the river bank. The kinship role in production is also reduced and the immediate family helps in the same way as in the schemes. The tenant in both the schemes, and in particular in the Suleim, has relative autonomy and theoretically, specially in the Suleim, owns his means of production where one owns his land and means of irrigation whether a *sagiya* or a small pump – a situation approximating to situation 'A' under the *sagiya* system. However, the constraints on the peasant cultivator here emanate from the control exercised by the traders over his produce through the *shayl* and mortgage relations (described in pages 59–60) to which the scheme tenant is also exposed but to a lesser degree. The tenants in both the schemes and the Suleim basin are subjected to the control of traders in the marketing of their produce, yet the type of organization described for the Suleim distinguished the latter whom I called peasant cultivators from the tenant cultivators in the schemes. The social organization of the Suleim peasants and those tenant cultivators scattered over numerous schemes is different. The main reason for that is the nature and mode of their agricultural production as independent units which present them as difficult to organize.[4]

However the changes in agricultural production have shown their influence on the ethnic relations of the Danagla groups in a manner comparable to those changes in the kinship organisation and its functions. The divisions among the groups were formerly based on genealogical differences and the history of settlement, as I have shown in Chapter Two, which separated the *non-ahali* from the ownership of land in the *milk*. The differences between them were used as economic differences identifying the two categories of 'haves' and 'have-nots' as *ahali* and non-*ahali* respectively; and this safeguarded *ahali* rights in their land from the competition of these groups especially when it was almost impossible to extend the land beyond the areas irrigable by the *sagiya*. So there was a form of division of labour which at the community level was based on the ethnic identification; *ahali* as cultivators, Falaliyh as traders and craftsmen, nomads as source of seasonal labour and Sudaniyya as domestic and agricultural labour for their ex-masters - and at the kinship group level on age and sex. With the expansion of agricultural production share-croppers were needed and this called for a type of co-operation cutting across kinship, ethnic and village allegiance. The ethnic divisions as depicted in the dichotomy *ahali*/non-*ahali*, no longer hold in the schemes as the former *ahali* peasants themselves changed into tenant cultivators together with non-*ahali* as share-croppers, *muzari'in* (See Table III, p.36). The same tendency is also working towards greater differentiation and mobility into different economic activities depending on individuals' resources, which no longer necessarily originate in agricultural work. Hence the possibility of classifying the Danagla as economic classes defined by their position vis-a-vis the means of production cutting across and above ethnic differences.

A question of theoretical interest arises here as to whether peasant and tenant cultivators can organize as a class bringing about social change by their political struggle against capital. As my data suggests there is a tendency for alignment along class interests - the Burgeig December case for example (see Chapter 5) but their organization for political action is far from being established here for the whole region. Abortive actions, like the one referred to above, do not precipitate considerable changes in the relations of production and the social structure of the Danagla at least at present. Nevertheless, and with the continuation of the present developments in agriculture, the alienation of the peasant/tenant cultivators from the means of production is increasing. When this is completed, the present forms of relations of production will change and a new set of relations will develop which will eventually intensify the polarization of peasants versus landlords/capitalists. At that point, an analysis based on political conflict between them will be feasible.

## Notes

1 See p.46
2 See Marx, K., *Wage, Labour and Capital*, Progress Publishers, p.28.
3 See p.13.
4 I did not deal with the present attempts of the Sudan Socialist Union to establish Farmers' Unions in the area, which proved a complete failure. However, there are three functioning Unions: one for the Burgeig Scheme; one supposed to be the Regional Union for tenants but representing the scheme owners instead; and the third for the Northern part.

# Appendix

*Glossary*

'A' stands for Arabic origin.
'N' stands for Nubian or Dongolese origin.

| | |
|---|---|
| *'abiyd (A):* | Sing. 'abd, slave. |
| *ahali (A):* | Indigenous or 'native' residents of a place. It stems from *ahal* which means 'relatives'. |
| *ansar (A):* | Disciples; followers of the Mahdi. |
| *aurwatti (N):* | A person sitting behind the animals driving the *sagiya* |
| *banat (A):* | (Sing. bint): daughter. Hence *bint 'am*, father's brother's daughter. |
| *burkij (N):* | Devastation. |
| *dammiyra (A):* | Nile flood. Hence the cultivating season. |
| *diywan (A):* | Guest-quarters for men belonging to a particular family. |
| *dolaig (N):* | Picking up of fallen ears of wheat when it is cut. |
| *dukhun (A):* | *Pennisetum typhoideum*. Bulrush millet. Used for making porridge. |
| *dulab (A):* | Wheel. |
| *dura (A):* | *Sorghum vulgare*. Great millet. |
| *faddan (A):* | A measure of area approximately 1.038 acres. |
| *faza'a (A):* | Communal work without cash reward. |
| *ful masri (A):* | Tick beans or horse beans. Introduced from Egypt (Misr). |
| *ga'ab (A):* | (Plural *Ga'ub*), oasis. |
| *gaddah (A):* | Literally a wooden bowl. It is used here for material exchanges in social occasions whereby people pay money or grain to help, expecting the recipient to reciprocate on similar occasions. |
| *garoora (A):* | Derives from *garra*, to draw. Credit account with a shop-keeper. |
| *hag-el-gusad (A):* | Right of frontage. |
| *haddam (A):* | Washing away of the river-banks. Lateral erosion. |
| *heiy (A):* | A residential quarter within a village or a town. |
| *jarf (A):* | Sloping patch of the river which is seasonally inundated. |
| *jiygol (N):* | A domestic and agricultural labourer. |
| *kasr (A):* | One hundredth of a *faddan* i.e. 42 sq.m. |
| *karoo (?)* | Land falling beyond the cultivated land. |
| *kayyal (A):* | A person who measures and sells grain. |
| *khashm (A):* | Pl. *khushum* – literally means 'mouth'. A fraction equal to $\frac{1}{12}$th of any unit for division |

*kiddaig (N):* Cutting the *dura* stables off the stalks after they are cut down.

*kodaig (N):* Excavation of the river bank below the *sagiya* or sucking pipe of a pump to remove sands obstructing water passage.

*lubiya (A):* *Dolichos lablab*: The plant is used as fodder for animals, and the seeds are boiled and eaten, especially in Ramadan.

*mariysa (A):* A beer of fermented dates. Also made of *dura* in central and other parts of the Sudan.

*matara (?):* (Plural *matarat*), a big well on which a *sagiya* or a small pump is installed for irrigation.

*milk (A):* Freehold.

*miyri (A):* *Amiyri*: belonging to the *amiyr*, prince of Egypt. The corrupted form *miyri* is still used to refer to government land.

*muhajiriyn (A):* Singular *muhajir*, emigrant. Name used for those Falaliyh who fled to Egypt in the Mahdiyya and came back after the Re-Conquest in 1898.

*mulukhiya (A):* *Corchorus olitorius* or Jew's mallow.

*muzari' (A):* (Plural *muzari'in*) Farmer. It means anyone who is involved in agriculture (*zira'a*), investors or cultivators alike. Now it has taken over from *turbal* to refer to those who undertake cultivation.

*nas (A):* People. But usually comes before a name of a person or place to refer to a group of relatives or neighbours.

*nafir (nafiyr) A:* Communal work group (see faza'a).

*noraj (?):* An animal-drawn threshing machine with disc-like wheels fitted to a wooden frame.

*onda (A):* A person of authority over a number of villages. In the system of Native Administration he was second from the bottom of the administrative hierarchy.

*rabiy' (A):* Spring. Hence *rabiy'i*, refers to crops grown in March–April especially *dura* and *lubiya* as fodder crops.

*rammiya (A):* Equivalent to *shayl* used in other parts of Sudan; a system of credit the payment of which necessitates the mortgage, or pricing in advance of the crops.

*sagiya (A):* Wooden water-wheel drawn by oxen (See plate 6). It also refers to the plot of land and the people owning it.

*saluka (A):* A digging stick used for making holes for seeds in wet land. Such land is also called *saluka* land.

*samad (A):* Agricultural supervisor and overseer for a plot of land (*samad moiya*). Also refers to the representative of the *sagiya owners* (*samad sagiya*).

*sayf (A):* Summer. Hence *sayfi, dura* which is cultivated in summer.

*shaduf (A):* Hand-operated lever with a bucket on the water side and counter weight on the other for raising water.

*shawiysh (?):* A sergeant.

*shaykh (A):* See *shayl.*

*shitta (A):* Winter. Hence *shitwi*, winter crops especially wheat.

*sug (A):* Market (-place).

*tagga (?):* Threshing place.

*tashash (A):* Petty trader (See Plate 10). Hence *tishasha*, petty trade.

*turbal (N):* (Plural *tarabla*) A person who actually undertakes cultivation - provides agricultural labour only.

# Bibliography

A — Government Publications and Local Official documents used
B — Published Works cited
C — Other sources of information or inspiration not cited


A — Government Publications and Local Official documents

1. *The Agricultural Bank of the Sudan, Dongola Branch:*
   — *Annual Reports* for the years 1965/66, 1966/67, 1967/68, 1968/69 and 1969/70
2. *Assistant Commissioner for Agricultural Affairs, Dongola*:
   — *Annual Reports*, 1964/65, 1965/66, 1966/67, 1967/68, 1968/69, 1969/70, 1970/71, 1971/72, 1972/73, 1973/74, 1975/76, and 1976/77
   — Memorandum on the obstacles of agricultural production in the Northern Province, 14.9.1976
   — *Kamneya Co-operative Scheme*, Mushu (File)
   — *Mushu Commercial Scheme* (File)
   — *Socio-Economic Survey of the Kerma - Suleim Basin*, by Tag el Sir Abdul Mutalib, Ministry of Agriculture, Khartoum, 1970
   — *The Suleim Basin*: Memorandum prepared for the Provincial Conference on 'The Future of Agricultural Production in the Northern Province' by Abdul Basit Mukhtar, Dongola, April 1976
3. *Assistant Commissioner for Co-operation, Dongola*:
   — *Annual Report* 1975/76
   — *Files* of the following Co-operative Schemes: Shaykh - Shariyf South, el-Tayiti, Sugdan, Koyya el-Aradayba, Sowri and Salagi
   — El-Khandaq Co-operative Union (General File) for:
   a. A Memorandum from the Manager to the Director, Co-operation Department, Khartoum, 1971
   b. A Memorandum addressed to the Director of Co-operation, Khartoum, and the Registrar of Co-operative Societies, 18.8.1972
4. *Department of Statistics, Khartoum*:
   — *First Population Census of the Sudan 1955/56, Final Report,* Vol. I.
   — *A Report on the Sample Census of Agriculture for the year 1964/65 in the Northern Provinces of the Sudan*, 1969.
5. *Dongola Peoples Rural Council, Dongola*:
   — *A Directory to Merowe-Dongola District* by H. M. A. Sharfi, 1957.
   — 1974 Population Census local statistics
   — *Village Councils* (general file)
6. *Land Registration Office, Dongola*:
   — *A Memorandum on the land registration*, 1964.
   — *Register of Agada Land*, 1972
7. *Sudan Gazette*, Khartoum:
   — *Land Registration Ordinance No. 29, The Nile Pump Control (General) Regulations*; A Memorandum to District Commissioners, 1964
   — No. 46, April 1903
   — *Unregistered Land Law, 1970, Legislative Supplement*, April 1970

8. *Sudan Collection, University of Khartoum*:
— *'Intelligence Reports'*, Egypt, January 1897
— 'Reports on the Province of Dongola', 1897 *Sudan Pamphlets*, Vol. 15

B — Published Works Cited in the text

Abu Salim, M. I., *al-Ard fi al-Mahdiyya*, Sudan Research Unit, University of Khartoum 1971
Adam, F. H., 'Patterns of Agricultural Production in the Sudan', *The Bulletin of Sudanese Studies*, 1972
Adam, F. H. et.al., *On the Modernization of Agricultural Production in the Northern Region (the Northern and Nile Provinces)*, Working Paper No. 24, The Arkowit Annual Conference, University of Khartoum, July 1976
Adams, W. Y., 'Continuity and Change in Nubian Cultural History', *Sudan Notes and Records*, Vol. 48, 1967
Ahmed, A. M., *Economic Anthropology and Problems of Development in the Sudan*, Khartoum University Press, 1975 (in Arabic)
Ahmed, A. H., 'Some Aspects Hampering the Development of Sudanese Trade during the 19th Century' *Sudan Journal of Economic and Social Studies*, Vol. 2, No. 1, 1977
Al-Shahi, A. S., *An Anthropological Study of a Northern Sudan Shaiqiya Village*; Unpublished Ph.D. Thesis, Oxford, 1971
Arkell, A. J., 'Dongola' in *Encyclopaedia Britannica*, Vol. 7, 1961
Barbour, K. M., *The Republic of the Sudan*, University of London Press, 1964
Bardeleben, M., *The Co-operative System in the Sudan*, München, 1973
Barnett, T., *The Gezira Scheme: An Illusion of Development*, MacMillan, London, 1977
Beshai, A. A., *Export Performance and Development in Sudan 1900*–1967, Ithaca Press, London, 1976
Boesnik, J., *On Peasants and the Modes of Production: Debate*, Project Paper No. A772, Centre for Development Research, Copenhagen, 1977
Bond, W. R. G., 'Some Curious Methods of Cultivation in Dongola Province', *Sudan Notes and Records*, Vol. 8, 1925.
Bradby, B., 'Destruction of the Natural Economy', *Economy and Society*, Vol. 4, No. 2, May 1975
Crawford, O. G. S., *The Fung Kingdom of Sennar*, Gloucester, 1951
Dafalla, H., 'Land Economy of Old Halfa', *Sudan Notes and Records*, Vol. 50, 1969
Dalton, G., 'Peasantries in Anthropology and History', *Current Anthropology*, Vol. 13, No. 3–4, June-October, 1972
Ennew, J., and Others, 'Peasantry as an Economic Category'; *Journal of Peasant Studies*, Vol. 4, No. 4, 1977
Frank, A. G., *Capitalism and Underdevelopment in Latin America*, Penguin - Harmondsworth, 1971

C — Other Sources of Information or Inspiration not cited in the text

Abdul Mageed, Y., *Rural Proletarians*, Shiykan Publishing House, Khartoum (n.d.)
Alavi, H., 'Peasant Classes and Primordial Loyalties', *Journal of Peasant Studies*, Vol. 1, No. 1, October 1973
Ali, A. A., *Some Aspects of Productivity in Sudanese Traditional Agriculture: the case of the Northern Province*: Bulletin No. 59, Economic and Social Research Council, Khartoum, 1977
Asad, T., 'Market Models, Class Structure and Consent: A Reconsideration of Swat Political Organization', *Man*, Vol. 7, No. 1, March, 1972

Barth, F., 'Models of Social Organization' Royal Anthropological Institute, Occasional Paper No. 23

Chayanov, A. V., *On the Theory of Peasant Economy*, Edited by D. Thorner, et.al., Illinois, 1966

Coquery-Vidrovitch, C., 'Research on an African Mode of Production' *Critique of Anthropology*, Nos. 4 and 5, Autumn, 1975

'The Political Economy of African Peasantry and Modes of Production' in, Peter C. W. Gutkind and I. Wallerstein (editors), *The Political Economy of Contemporary Africa.* Sage Publications, London, 1976

Cutler, A., 'The Concept of Ground Rent and Capitalism in Agriculture' *Critique of Anthropology*, Nos. 4–5, Autumn, 1975

Dalton, G., 'Peasant Markets', *Journal of Peasant Studies*, Vol. 1, No. 4, 1974

'Theoretical Issues in Economic Anthropology', *Current Anthropology*, Vol. 10, No. 1, Feb., 1969

Davey, B., 'Modes of Production, Socio-Economic Formations, Combined and Uneven Development', *South Asia Marxist Review*, Vol. 1, No. 2

Emmanual, A., *'Unequal Exchange: a Study in the Imperialism of Trade'*, New Left Books, London, 1972

Frank, A. G., *Sociology of Development and Underdevelopment of Sociology*, Pluto Press, London, 1973

Harrison, M., 'The Peasant Mode of Production in the Work of A. V. Chayanov', *Journal of Peasant Studies*, Vol. 4, No. 4, 1977

Hassan, Y. F., *The Arabs and the Sudan*, Khartoum University Press, 1973

Hay, R., Jr., and J. Abu Lughod (editors) *Third World Urbanization*, Chicago, 1977

Hewison, J. W., 'Northern Province Agriculture' in *Agriculture in the Sudan*, edited by J. D. Tothill, Oxford, 1952

Hobsbawm, E., 'Introduction' to Karl Marx, *Pre-Capitalist Economic Formations*, Lawrence and Wishart, London, 1975

Holt, P. M., *A Modern History of the Sudan*, London, 1963

Holy, L., *Neighbours and Kinsmen: a Study of the Berti People of Darfur*, London, 1974

International Labour Office, *Growth, Employment and Equity: a Comprehensive Strategy for the Sudan*, Vol. 2, Geneva, October 1975

Kay, G., *Development and Underdevelopment: a Marxist Analysis*, London, 1977

Kronenberg, A. and W., 'Parallel Cousin Marriage in Medieval and Modern Nubia', Part 2, *Kush*, Vol. 13, 1965

Laclau, E., 'Feudalism and Capitalism in Latin America', *New Left Review*, No. 67, 1971

Leach, T. A., 'Date-Trees in Halfa Province' *Sudan Notes and Records*, Vol. 2, No. 2, 1919

Leaver, R., 'The Debate on Underdevelopment: "On Situating Gunder Frank"', *Journal of Contemporary Asia*, Vol. 7, No. 1, 1977

Long, N., *An Introduction to the Sociology of Rural Development*, Tavistock, 1977

MacMichael, H. A., *A History of the Arabs in the Sudan*, Vol. 1, Cass, London, 1967

Marx, K., *Grundrisse: Introduction to the Critique of Political Economy*, Pelican Books, 1973

Nicholls, W., 'The Sakia (Sagiya) in Dongola Province', *Sudan Notes and Records*, Vol. 1, 1918

Omer, E. A. B., *Peasantry and Social Change in a Northern Sudanese Community: A Study of a Danagla Village, Mushu*, Unpublished M.Sc. Thesis, University of Khartoum, 1975

*Rural Traders and Socio-Economic Transformation in Dongola Area, Northern Province*, Bulletin No. 47, Economic and Social Research Council, Khartoum, 1976

Purves, W. D. C. L., 'Some Aspects of the Northern Province' in J. A. de C. Hamilton (editor). The Anglo-Egyptian Sudan from Within, London, 1935

Redfield, R., *Peasant Society and Culture*, Chicago, 1956

*Review of African Political Economy*, No. 3, May-October, 1975, 'Editorial'
Salih, G. M., 'The Heritage of Local Government' in *Local Government and Politics in the Sudan*, edited by J. Howell, Khartoum University Press, 1974
Shamin, T., 'The Nature and Logic of the Peasant Economy; 1: a Generalization', *Journal of Peasant Studies*, Vol. 1, No. 1, 1973
Shaw, D. J. 'The Development and Contribution of Irrigated Agriculture in the Sudan' in, *Agricultural Development in the Sudan*, Vol. 2, Papers for the 13th Annual Conference of the Philosophical Society of the Sudan, Khartoum, 1966
'The Effects of Money-lending (Sheil) on Agricultural Development in the Sudan' in D. J. Shaw (ed.) *ibid.*
Thornton, S., 'Regional Development: the Case of the Northern Sudan' in D. J. Shaw (ed.) *ibid.*
Wilmington, M. W., 'Aspects of Money-lending in Northern Sudan' *The Middle East Journal*, 1955
Wolf, E., *Peasants*, Prentice-Hall, New Jersey, 1966
*Peasant Wars of the Twentieth Century*, Faber and Faber, 1969
Wynn, R. F., *The Development, Present Economic Performance and Future Prospects of Nile Pump Irrigated Agriculture in Sudan*, University of Khartoum, 1967